DINING
WITH THE
IMPRESSIONISTS

Jocelyn Hackforth-Jones

DINING
WITH THE
IMPRESSIONISTS

with thirty recipes by
Hélène and Didier Gans

KONECKY&KONECKY

ACKNOWLEDGMENTS

I would like to thank the following people: Penny Wesson, Martin Nield, Tessa Kerwood, Pom Oliver, Anne Dewe, Pennie Alfrey, Nicholas Alfrey, Caroline Bugler, and Jonathan Watkins. I am grateful to Margaret Walters for reading and commenting on the text, for sharing her ideas, and for her enthusiasm for the project. I am indebted to Michael Jacobs for his generous assistance and advice and for lending me his excellent *Guide to Provence* (Penguin, 1989). I would also like to record an additional debt to Sally Kindberg for her support and encouragement.

Finally, I want to thank my mother, Susan Hackforth-Jones, for a lifetime of delicious cooking, for her stimulating conversations about food, and for continuing and passing on her own "cuisine grand-mère."

Konecky & Konecky
156 Fifth Avenue
New York, New York 10010

CONTENTS

INTRODUCTION: Dining with the Impressionists

Eating and drinking, taking meals together, picnicking, and cooking all played an important role in the lives and art of Impressionist painters. In the years leading up to the first Impressionist exhibition in 1874, many of these artists lived or had studios in Montmartre or the Batignolles district of Paris. As well as meeting informally in their studios, they congregated in their favorite local cafés. Paris was expanding and restaurants and cafés proliferated. Toward the end of the century as these avant-garde artists became successful, they got together in more expensive restaurants, where they could taste the delights of haute cuisine. It is no coincidence that the emergence, in Europe's premier modern city, of an art that was consciously modern in style and subject matter was paralleled by the development of modern cooking exemplified by the cuisine of Auguste Escoffier.

The paintings represent an ongoing record of the Impressionists' enjoyment of food. Many consistently returned to still life as a subject for the sensuous representation of fruits, vegetables, meat, fish, game, wines, preserves, and pastries. They painted ordinary get-togethers in cafés, brasseries, and inns, and depicted domestic entertainments that ranged from informal family dinners and simple meals with friends, to more

☐

Detail from page 9

formal and elegant occasions set in darkened rooms, such as Gustave Caillebotte's *Luncheon*. Some depicted the fashionable rituals of tea drinking both at home and in the newly built salons de thé.

In the middle of the nineteenth century, Paris became a burgeoning industrialized metropolis—a development accompanied by the rapid growth of a leisure and entertainment industry backed by ambitious entrepreneurs. Parisians' lifestyles experienced a similar shift: leisure and pleasure activities became increasingly available to a larger group of people that included the working classes.

In the works of these modern artists, mealtimes and refreshment were relaxed, jovial occasions drawn from contemporary life. Breakfasts, lunches, and dinners (both public and private) were painted in and around Paris, showing everyone gathered casually around a table or enjoying a picnic. They painted the new and popular music halls, cafés, and restaurants around Montmartre. Renoir suggested something of the gaiety, the flirting, and the press of people when he pictured his friends enjoying themselves in *Ball at the Moulin de la Galette* and *La Fin du*

Pierre-Auguste Renoir, *Ball at the Moulin de la Galette*, 1876
Paris, Musée d'Orsay

Here Renoir pictures a Sunday dance at the open-air dance hall attached to the windmill on the top of the butte Montmartre. He wanted to communicate the atmosphere and jollity of these occasions frequented by local people on their day off. Most of the fore- and middleground characters were artist and writer friends, talking to or dancing with the local girls whom they employed as models.

Pierre-Auguste Renoir, *The Rowers'
Luncheon*, 1879
Chicago, Art Institute

This is one of a series of paintings
that Renoir made focusing on
rowing along the Seine, probably
near the island of Chatou. Here we
have a suburban version of *The End
of Lunch*. The airy, relaxed mood,
evident in the subject and the poses
of the diners, is repeated in the
handling of paint. The long brush
strokes blending into each other in
the foreground have a sensuous
appeal that is reiterated in the
slightly blurred still life.

déjeuner (*The End of Lunch*). Alfresco dining also figured in the Impressionists' subject matter, as one would expect from artists committed to modern life subjects and to painting in the open air. They painted picnics in the recently developed Bois de Boulogne, along the banks of the Seine, and further afield at Fontainebleau and Barbizon. Both Renoir and Monet depicted plein air meals; Renoir painted his Parisian visitors dining on a restaurant terrace overlooking the Seine, lazy and replete in *Le Dejeuner des canotiers* (*Luncheon of the Boating Party*), or boatmen after a summer lunch overlooking the Seine in *The Rowers' Luncheon*.

Built into the notion of leisure and pleasure was the sense of nostalgia, for these joys were only fleetingly available in work's off-hours: eating and drinking, boating, picnicking, and dancing were activities to be savored on one's day off. The last stages or end of a meal was a subject the

9

Impressionists returned to time and again, showing the table littered
with half-empty wine glasses, coffee cups, fruit, and bread in an attempt
to capture a fleeting moment. In *Luncheon* (1873) Monet pictured the
remains of an outdoor meal on a summer's day in the garden at Argenteuil where he lived after his marriage to his first wife, Camille. The
remains of fruit, coffee, and bread and the full-blown rose (which will

**Claude Monet, *Luncheon*, c. 1873
Paris, Musée d'Orsay**

Monet moved to Argenteuil at the end of 1871 with
his wife Camille and son Jean, where he established a
prosperous middle-class home in the suburbs. He
rented a house and set about planting a flower garden, which with the remains of a summer lunch, are
featured in this painting where he has captured a
brief idyllic moment.

soon wither) lying on the abandoned table in the midst of his garden in bloom, are all powerful indications of the transitoriness of this moment and of the evanescent quality of sensory pleasures. Anyone who cooks knows how quickly the moment of delight in the sight, smells, texture, and taste of a carefully prepared meal fades, so that all one is left with are the remains on the table.

There may also have been some practical considerations in depicting the last stages or end of a meal, since it was easier for the artists to determine figural groupings in this way than if everyone had a table "placement." The end of a meal also presented narrative possibilities; as in Manet's *Chez le père Lathuille,* where we are left wondering whether the woman will accept the man's proposition. The finale of the meal has suggestive overtones.

For the Impressionists, the representation of the remains of meal also provided an opportunity to display their mastery of still life detail. Monet

and Renoir used a few rapid strokes to suggest peaches, grapes, and the leftover bread and wine that are vital parts of their paintings' sensuous attraction. Manet also used still life detail to add to a work's meaning, as in his *Le Déjeuner sur l'herbe.* The bread, basket of fruit, figs, and cherries laid out on the discarded dress of the nude woman have obvious sexual connotations and provide an ironic and witty commentary on the subject

11

Detail from page 12

Édouard Manet, *Le Déjeuner sur l'herbe*, 1863
Paris, Musée d'Orsay

Manet's exhibition of this painting
outraged public and critics alike. In
spite of the fact that Manet was
reworking a traditional subject, his
contemporaries objected to the fact
that the men were in modern dress
and that the woman's
confrontational stance and stare did
not conform to accepted notions of
female beauty. They also felt that
the handling of paint lacked polish
and refinement. One of Manet's
favorite models, Victorine Meurent,
posed for the woman, and his
brother and brother-in-law
(Ferdinand Leenhoff) were the
models for the men. The woman is
clearly a prostitute, and Manet's
sense of irony is evident in the way
in which the fruit acts as a
metaphor for sexual exchange,
lying as it does on the discarded
dress of the nude.

at hand. The painting itself is a mixture of the historical and the contemporary or real. Referring to an engraving after Raphael of the *Judgment of Paris* for the poses of the two men and to Titian's *The Concert* (c. 1508), which depicts clothed men with nude women in a sylvan setting accompanied by music, Manet's painting provides a contemporary element in the pose of the woman and in the artist's antiacademic handling. Similarly, the fruit has time-honored historical associations, reminding us of the fall of man at the hands of a woman/temptress like the nude in the foreground; but the fruit is also "real," reminding us that the ostensible purpose of this get-together was to picnic.

In their paintings of still lifes, the Impressionists chose traditional subject matter that had been enjoying a general revival in France since the middle of the century. Middle-class art buyers wanted small paintings that would fit into their domestic environment and did not carry the complex references of historical painting. There was a renewed interest in the still life and genre paintings of Jean-Baptiste Chardin, and some artists like Henri Fantin-Latour were able to make successful careers working within this tradition. Artists like Eugène Boudin turned to the painting of still lifes for financial reasons: as a result of commissions from regional middle-class collectors.

They were of course aware of this history and of the way in which seventeenth-century Dutch still life painters had exploited to the full a subtle system of coding: for instance, what appeared to be a straightforward arrangement of flowers and overripe fruit interspersed with treasured objects was both a celebration of the artist's skill in realistic representation and an essay on the notion of *vanitas*, or the transience of life. The moral behind the work warned of attaching too much importance to worldly possessions. Seventeenth-century Dutch still lifes were primarily allegorical and sociological in nature, while the Impressionists expressed their nostalgia for the fleeting pleasures of eating and drinking in a busy urban world.

Within this context there is considerable variation in their treatment of the subject. Monet's still lifes capture shifting effects of light and color, while both Gauguin and Cézanne used still life as a means of experimenting with novel ways of suggesting forms in space.

For Manet still life was an important training ground for the artist and served to comment on his notion of the "real." His still lifes have a physical, sensuous presence. In the simple paintings of one still life object—ham, asparagus, lemon, or fish—he manages to convey at once its substance and tangible appeal so that it becomes immediately "real" to the viewer. In *A Bunch of Asparagus* we focus on the asparagus positioned in the foreground. It is painted with swift thin strokes that catch the eye and seem to bring it closer to the viewer—an effect that is further enhanced by the way in which the asparagus spears are dramatically highlighted and set against a dark, densely painted background. The strength of Manet's paintings of food lies in their deceptively simple compositions and in his handling of paint. They focus on everyday foods that Manet himself regularly ate and enjoyed. He attached great significance to the painting of still lifes, claiming that they were the touchstone of the painter.[1]

On occasion Manet painted more elaborate still lifes, perhaps with an eye to augmenting his sales, in light of the increasing reputation of artists such as Philippe Rousseau, whose elegant still lifes were popular with the affluent bourgeoisie. Manet often presented a number of objects laid out on a white tablecloth against a plain (generally dark) background. Very often the compositional arrangement was deliberate and formalized, with the tablecloth folded over, a knife set at an angle, and a lemon placed toward the edge of the table. In *Still Life with Fish* and *Fruits on a Table,* this studied disposition of fish and fruits is offset by the vivacity of the paint work. Furthermore, the tablecloth acts as a lightening agent and lifts both the tones and the colors of the painting, adding to the naturalism of the works.

Manet's still lifes reflect his concern with *la vie moderne* just as much as his portraits and scenes of leisure and entertainment set in the cafés, parks, and pleasure domes of contemporary Paris. Very often, owing to his original placement of forms and subtle handling of lighting and color effects, these subjects have a material presence. Manet's enjoyment of still life is clear from the painter Charles Tòché's description of his stay

in Venice in 1874. Apparently Manet was particularly excited by visits to the vegetable and fish market, where he was taken by the light and color reflecting from the scales of the fish. Dining with him at a little restaurant opposite the Giudecca, Toché noted: "Manet observed and analyzed the different colors taken on by each object as the light faded. He defined

Édouard Manet, *A Bunch of Asparagus*, c. 1880
Cologne, Wallraf-Richartz Museum

Manet's vibrant study of the asparagus here connects with his interest in contemporary subject matter and with finding ways to suggest the material presence of the objects and people that he painted. Here the ordinary and the everyday is made real to us by the fluent handling of paint: thin strokes of pigment have been rapidly applied so that the painting takes on a sketch-like immediacy.

their values, and told us how he would try to reproduce them, steeped in this ashy twilight greyness."[2]

Manet's appreciation of still life was an integral part of his daily existence. He loved not only the objects themselves but also the subtle transformation that they underwent under different conditions of light.

Avant-garde contemporaries such as Camille Pissarro and Gustave Caillebotte also had both a literal and an artistic devotion to the markets. Pissarro's paintings of markets generally depicted the wider context: housewives poring over displays of meat and fish in search of freshness and good value. He recreated the activity there, the conversation, keen scrutiny, and careful selection that was part and parcel of any provincial market day and with which he became intimately familiar when working at Pontoise and Éragny. Caillebotte on the other hand exulted in the gorgeous displays of fruits in patterns of commercial exhibition. *Fruits à l'étalage* demonstrates the care and artistry of Parisian stall holders. The composition is given over to the portrayal of the different fruits dis-

17

Gustave Caillebotte, *Fruits à l'étalage*, 1880–1882
(detail)
Boston, Museum of Fine Arts

This dazzling display of fruit on a market stall testifies to Caillebotte's interest in still life and the marketplace as contemporary subject matter. In addition he appears to be interested in the shapes and colors of the different fruits against a backdrop of blue-white paper and the juxtaposition of warm and cool colors so that we also read the painting in terms of these patterns.

played against a backdrop of white paper. There is no suggestion of anything extraneous, no horizon line to give a sense of place and depth, only some lush dark green leaves to offset the riot of subtropical color: tomatoes, pears, lemons, berries, and figs. We read the painting as a series of interrelated shapes and colors designed in such a way as to maximize their sensual appeal. In many ways the work prefigures the more deliberately flat and decorative still lifes by artists such as Gauguin. Monet's freely handled still lifes such as *Pears and Grapes* take us in a different direction, away from the rigid structure and deliberation of

20

Claude Monet, *Pears and Grapes*, 1880
Hamburg, Kunsthalle

Page 21: detail

Monet's still lifes effectively broke with the Chardin tradition of carefully structured realist still life painting to produce a definitively "Impressionist" approach, both in the informality of the composition and in the way he sets separate strokes of vibrant color against a lighter tan ground. In paintings like these Monet suggests the fleeting nature of sensuous pleasure.

traditional still life painting exemplified by Chardin. There is a casual, almost disordered quality in the way the pears and grapes seem to spill across the canvas and in the handling of paint—the gestural brushwork in which separate brush strokes create a skein of texture and fractured light effects. At this time (roughly between 1878 and 1882) Monet turned to still life painting since he was able to sell these more easily than his landscapes.

Paul Cézanne, *Still Life with Soup Tureen,* 1877
Paris, Musée d'Orsay

Here Cézanne, concerned with suggesting the individual solidity of each object, uses a system of parallel brush strokes known as his "constructive" stroke. The physical presence of the apples is enhanced by Cézanne's use of complementaries so that the red-yellow and orange of the apples are offset by touches of blue. This technique is also used in the soup tureen and tablecloth.

Many of Cézanne's still lifes have a sensory perspective which here reflects the precise relationship between artist and object at a given moment (before he moved on to the next object seen from a different angle). We are therefore left with many deliberate inconsistencies and ambiguities in scale and perspective. The size of the plaster cast of a Cupid (which may still be seen in Cézanne's studio in Aix), which in reality was only eighteen inches high, is exaggerated, as is the onion to the left of the statue and the apple in the background.

Cézanne's approach to still life was different again. For him it was the perfect subject since it enabled him to choose and compare objects with reference to the natural world without having to worry about the inconsistencies of nature. Initially he adopted a frontal focus before an arrangement of objects, as in *Still Life with Soup Tureen,* in which he established a sense of the density of the fruit within their contours by means of a system of parallel brush strokes—his so-called constructive stroke. In his later compositions the still life was arranged and built up with equal care. One young artist, Louis le Bail, watching Cézanne set up a still life in the late 1890s described the way in which he carefully laid a cloth on the table before arranging the fruits so that one tone contrasted with another and the complementaries vibrated against each other: red/green, yellow/purple, and blue/orange: "He brought to this task the greatest care and many precautions: one guessed that it was a feast for the eye to him."[3] Many of Cézanne's still lifes substitute what could be called a sensory perspective for a traditional one. We are left with varying viewpoints within the one picture, as in *Still Life with Plaster Cast*. The differences in proportion did not worry him, since he aimed for a harmony of colored relationships rather than illusionistic representation.

Not only did food and drink play an important role in the subject matter of the Impressionists, but the delights of the table formed a significant part of their daily life, from their earliest days as student artists into their mature years of recognition and prosperity. In *L'Oeuvre* (1886) Émile Zola described an end-of-term feast at a studio, based on the Académie Suisse frequented by Manet, Monet, and Pissarro: "By midnight they had stuffed themselves with brawn, saveloy, and other cheap food washed down with quarts of vin ordinaire. Toward one o'clock they had secured the company of some 'ladies,' and without the work abating the feast had turned into a Roman orgy, combined with a smoking marathon. On the damp, stained floor there remained a great litter of greasy paper and broken bottles, while the atmosphere reeked of burnt tallow, cheap scent, highly seasoned sausages, and wine."[4]

When they were young and poor the artists ate in cafés, cheap restaurants, and guinguettes, or suburban taverns—a coinage probably derived from *guinguet*, the grape used to make the sour but cheap wine frequently drunk there. Originally situated on the outskirts of Paris, the guinguettes were often located in attractive surroundings where customers could go to eat, drink, and dance. The food was essentially plain fare: bread and soup or a steaming pot-au-feu. The cheaper restaurants in Montmartre were known for their cuisine bourgeoise—good substantial home cooking with a staple casserole that was kept going on the stove all day. A typical meal consisted of meat, vegetables, salad, and dessert. This was also the kind of board offered to artists in restaurants and inns outside Paris, such as Ravoux's restaurant at Auvers-sur-Oise, which housed van Gogh toward the end of his life.

The middle classes had only begun to frequent restaurants following the French Revolution in 1789. Around 1765 Monsieur Boulanger, a Parisian soup merchant, opened the first modern restaurant, complete with bare marble-topped tables. By the end of the eighteenth century there were five hundred restaurants in Paris alone, and one hundred years later restaurants of all kinds were to be found throughout Paris. Before the arrival of Auguste Escoffier, who came to Paris in 1870, the greatest French chef was Marie-Antoine Carême, the founder (in the first years of the nineteenth century) of French grande cuisine.

Carême was the acknowledged master of complex architectural virtuosities that would take up the centerpiece of a table, together with a "spec-

tacle" of heavy silver, with meats, desserts, and pastries served on elaborate structures reminiscent of famous statues. It was not uncommon for guests to encounter more than one hundred dishes at a sitting, many of which had cooled by the time they got to them.

English visitors commented on the length and quantity of the meals in France (although they often mistook the midday *déjeuner* for the morning's *petit déjeuner*). One traveler, the Reverend George Musgrave, who later published his account in *A Ramble through Normandy* in 1855, marveled at the unnatural "voracity and powers of assimilation" of the people he encountered and described a lunch eaten by a recently married couple: "I witnessed the first onslaught (when the soup was disposed of) upon the

25

Vincent van Gogh, *Still Life with Mackerel,* **1886**
Winterthur, collection of Oskar Reinhart

In this work painted when van Gogh was living in
Montmartre, the dark tones are enlivened by the
contrast between the bright red of the tomatoes and
the pure yellow of the lemons.

fried mackerel: it was a vigorous attack; but the fish bones, at any rate, were removed. Two relais of beefsteak, ditto of French beans and fried potatoes followed, with an omelette aux fines herbes, flanked immediately by a fricandeau of veal and sorrel; and these . . . were supplaced by a roast chicken garnished with mushrooms, commended to the gentle senses by a hock of ham served upon spinach. This engrossed an interval of twenty-five minutes—the chicken, indeed, having become invisible in the first ten . . . Then came an open apricot tart, three custards, and an endive salad, which I felt sure was the precursor of a small roast leg of lamb, with chopped onion and nutmeg powder sprinkled upon it. Then came the coffee and two glasses of absinthe and eau dorée, a Mignon cheese, pears, plums, grapes, and cakes—the two bottles of petit Bourgogne and one of Chablis having been emptied between eleven and one o'clock."[5]

Although people still continued to eat large meals at the end of the century (particularly in the provinces), Escoffier changed the very nature of classic French cooking. He cut down on the number of dishes and based his menus on healthy, easily digestible food. He did away with the practice of preparing meat in flour or boiling it, using instead three basic stocks as the basis of his cuisine. A typical Escoffier menu consisted of a first course of soup or melon, followed by a fish or shellfish specialty, then a meat dish and possibly some poultry before the vegetables, which were followed by dessert.

Although it is difficult to talk of a specifically Parisian cuisine, one can speak of a style of classic French cooking developed in Paris at the end of the nineteenth century. Escoffier was a crucial figure in this modernizing process. Born in Provence in 1846, he served his apprenticeship at his uncle's restaurant in Nice. He then divided his time between Paris and the south of France before entering into partnership with César Ritz. In 1890 they opened the Savoy Hotel in London and, in 1898, took charge of the kitchens at the Carlton Hotel.

Escoffier was instrumental in promoting regional recipes that were an integral part of the new cuisine. The Provençal dishes in his repertoire gained general currency via his publications, of which the best known are *Le Guide culinaire* (1903) and *Le Livre des menus* (1912). Many of his clients were appalled to discover that some of this dishes contained garlic, which they regarded as being too strong and crude in flavor and as having unwelcome associations with peasant cooking.

He was, then, the father of modern French cuisine. Many of his most famous dishes were served in Parisian restaurants frequented by the

Impressionists. During the 1870s and 1880s some of the group patronized the cheap restaurants of Montmartre; others, who were a little better off, preferred finer and more expensive establishments. Père Lathuille's, in the Batignolles district, was renowned for its poulet en cocotte. Those dishes that became part of the classic repertory of Parisian cuisine were labeled "à la parisienne."

Open-air restaurants and the café-concerts around the Champs-Elysée counted Manet and Degas among their clients. Le Doyen became particularly famous. It was there that artists and art lovers dined on the opening day of the Salon. The restaurant was justly famed for its fine food and extensive wine list.

Degas was a habitué of les Ambassadeurs and l'Alcazar. These open-air restaurants held concerts that he often painted. They both were superb restaurants; culinary guides of the time made note of the exceptionally fine champagne served at les Ambassadeurs.

A typical menu served to a small group at the end of the nineteenth century shows the influence of Escoffier.

Melon
Potage Ambassadeurs
Hors-d'oeuvre
Truite en Gelée Mâconnaise
Ris de Veau Financière
Demi-Vierge en Chaud-Froid
Poulets de Grain Rôtis
Salade de Romaine
Asperges Froides
Coupes Jacques
Dessert
Petites Fraises

Journée Sarah Bernhardt

MENU
DU
9 DÉCEMBRE
1896

From the 1880s as they became more successful, artists like Monet and Renoir could afford to indulge their taste in haute cuisine in some of the best restaurants in Paris and the south of France. Between 1880 and 1894 many of the Impressionists met at the Café Riche on the first Thursday of every month. Another of Monet's favorite restaurants at this time was the Café Anglais on the boulevard des Italiens, famed for its wine cellar and for (among other dishes) Pommes Anna (see recipe), which was created by the chef Adolphe Dugléré and dedicated to Anna Deslions, a woman of fashion during the Second Empire. Monet and the art critic Gustave Geffroy also instituted Friday dinners at the Hôtel Drouant in 1887. Some years later when his friend Marie-Ernest Richardin was compiling a book of recipes, Geffroy wrote and described these evenings: "They wanted a few hours of relaxation, freedom, conversation about everything, everyone speaking at once, agreeing, disagreeing, dreaming beautiful dreams, being by turn or simultaneously philosophers and little boys."[6]

Joining the artists at these dinners were writers, journalists, and politicians. Edmond de Goncourt, Rodin, Toulouse-Lautrec, and Paul Clemenceau were regulars. Drouant's house specialities included the hotel's own specially prepared champignons, woodcock, and thrush and its presentation of Lobster à l'Americaine and potage àu vin. Also served was Escoffier's innovative Salade Japonaise, a fruit salad made with pineapple, oranges, tomatoes, lettuce hearts, and fresh cream.

By the end of the century there was increasing interaction between

□

Le Café Anglais
Paris, Bibliothèque Nationale,
Cabinet des Estampes

The Café Anglais was set up on the boulevard des Italiens in 1802 and named in honor of the Peace of Amiens. It was noted for the excellence of its cuisine, and during the Second Empire its famous chef, Adolphe Dugléré created (among other dishes) Pommes Anna there. In the 1890s Monet and Madame Hoschedé were regular visitors.

□

Le Café Riche
Paris, Bibliothèque Nationale, Cabinet des Estampes

The Café Riche was opened on the boulevard des Italiens in 1804. Between 1880 and 1894 many Impressionist artists met there regularly on the first Thursday of every month.

provincial and metropolitan cuisines. Escoffier and Ritz can also be credited with raising the standard of cooking along the Riviera, which was fast becoming the site of the great hotels that attracted an international clientele. In the succeeding chapters we shall consider the development of Impressionist art with its commitment to modernity in style and subject matter: an art interwoven with emerging modern Paris. One of the key features of the new city was its cafés, which played a literal and figural role in the evolution of the new art. The Impressionists also referred to their domestic lives for subject matter. This is particularly true for the women artists who exhibited in the Impressionist shows but could not frequent the cafés.

Many of the Impressionists traveled widely through France in search of different landscape subjects, taking advantage of the network of railways that by the final quarter of the nineteenth century connected Paris with the most remote regions of the country. They went primarily to paint the landscapes of Normandy, Brittany, and Provence. We will find that once they went beyond the environs of Paris, their subject matter focused less on food and mealtimes and more on the landscapes.

Monet and Renoir frequently consulted contemporary guidebooks when searching for landscape sites. Initially the Impressionists stayed in favored inns or took lodgings at places such as the Saint-Siméon farm in Normandy or the Gloanec inn in Brittany. As they grew older and wealthier, they opted to stay in the more comfortable hotels, which offered superlative cuisine. There were gourmet guides to assist in making the right decisions. Monet and Renoir enjoyed such comforts when they stayed at Nice and Menton. As a wealthy bourgeoise, Berthe Morisot traveled all over the country in search of new and contemporary subjects, often accompanied by her husband and daughter. She stayed with family and friends, in hotels, and during the winter of 1881–1882, rented a house in the south of France. This spacious villa, the Villa Ratti, was situated on a hill overlooking Nice and was surrounded by large garden of olive, orange, fig, and pepper trees, with a thicket of bamboo and aloe. Morisot wrote to her sister Edma of their blooming health, both as a result of the restorative qualities of the climate and landscape, and also owing to the deliciousness of the cuisine niçoise. Every day they lunched in the garden, and that morning had gone to buy *bella sardina*.

For all these artists, as for the modern traveler today, the fascination of exploring new landscapes and cultures was accompanied by the pleasurable anticipation of discovering unfamiliar wines, ciders, or pastis, together with the joys of the local cuisine.

Detail from page 49

1

Impressionism was conceived in a café; some, like George Moore, went even further and declared that the café was "the real French acad-

PARIS AND THE SEINE

emy." It is fitting that avant-garde artists, committed to the notion of modernity in subject matter and approach, should have opted to get together in the cafés, brasseries, and restaurants that by the 1870s had become such a characteristic feature of metropolitan life.

The first café in the modern sense was the Café Procope established in 1696 by an Italian. It boasted chandeliers, the marble tables that were to

Camille Pissarro, *L'Avenue de l'Opéra*, 1898
Reims, Musée des Beaux-Arts

**Like many of the Impressionists, Pissarro painted
modern Paris. In this painting he conveys the new
sense of space provided by Baron Haussmann's wide
boulevards and sidewalks lined with café terraces.**

become ubiquitous in the nineteenth century, Italian sorbets and ices, and a counter selling confectionery. But it was not until the 1850s that cafés flourished, stimulated by Baron Haussmann's rebuilding of Paris. By 1872 when Marc Constantin published his history of the cafés and *cafés-concerts*, he complained: "Cafés have invaded the boulevards, concerts have invaded the cafés, and crowds have invaded everywhere to the great joy of the barkeepers who are getting rich." Certainly the cafés catered not only to native Parisians (who could if they wished begin and end their days in them), but also to increasing numbers of visitors to Paris. They ranged from dimly lit unadorned hostelries to brilliant establishments of mirror and glass that made use of the spacious streets and boulevards to include *terrasses* from which one could view the "theatre of the streets." By the end of the nineteenth century there were 24,000 cafés in the greater Paris area, each with its own individual character. Some catered to people from particular regions, while others were frequented by particular classes, professions, and political groups. As far as the arts, writing, philosophy, and journalism were concerned, the cafés supplanted eighteenth century salons as venues for the exchange of new ideas: for talking and arguing in conducive surroundings. Cafés were places to meet, smoke, and drink—not only coffee and wine, but also the increasingly sought-after absinthe and beer, as well as Grog Américain, a refreshing mixture of rum and water.

There were, too, the new brasseries and the café-concerts, which were (as the name implies) also places of musical entertainment ranging in size and scale. The east end of the Champs-Élysées was redeveloped and adorned with a circus, a building for displaying panoramas, two restaurants, two ice cream stalls, a cake stall, an open-air refreshment buffet, a bandstand, and three café-concerts, of which the Alcazar d'Été and the Ambassadors drew the largest crowds. Cafés-concerts attracted Impressionist painters as centers of urban life.

The Café Guerbois became the favorite meeting place for avant-garde artists in the late 1860s. Though Thursday was the preferred evening, they frequently got together on other days as well. Manet was the intellectual leader of the group. He had abandoned the terrace of the fashionable Café de Bade in the center of Paris for the Café Guerbois, where he was joined by artists and their friends, including some of the leading literary figures of the day. Renoir, Degas, and Fantin-Latour together with Bazille and Felix Bracquemond were frequent artist guests. Zola and the famous photographer and balloonist Nadar (in whose studio at the boulevard des Capucines the first Impressionist exhibition was held) would drop in occasionally, and Monet, Cézanne, Pissarro, and Sisley would join them whenever they were in Paris (at this time, they were often working outside Paris). Monet later recalled: "Nothing could have been more stimulating than the regular discussions that we used to have there with their constant clashes of opinion. . . . From them we emerged with stronger determination and with our thoughts clearer and more sharply defined."

Pierre-Auguste Renoir, *Au café*, 1877
Otterlo, Rijksmuseum Kröller-Müller

The sensuous appeal of color and brushwork is here also a metaphor for the intended appeal of the women, shown here being admired by the men. Our attention is drawn to them by the richness and texture of brush strokes on the woman's dress, face, and hair, and by the way in which Renoir uses blue/orange complementaries so that the deep blue dress stands out against the surrounding orange/gold strokes.

The location of the Café Guerbois in the Batignolles quarter was significant, for Batignolles was the first name given to that group of artists who made up the Impressionist movement. Manet lived at the boulevard des Batignolles, and his studio was nearby in the rue de Saint-Petersbourg. Renoir, Bazille, and Mallarmé also lived in this district.

Around 1875 there was a general move away from the Café Guerbois (probably at the instigation of the artist Marcellin Desboutin, who found it too noisy) to the Nouvelle-Athènes at the Place Pigalle in the neighboring quarter of Montmartre. The artistic clientele at the Nouvelle-Athènes included Jean-François Raffaelli, who was to exhibit in two Impressionist exhibitions. There was also Manet's former model, Victorine Meurent (who had posed for *Le Déjeuner sur l'herbe* in 1863), and the actress Ellen Andrée later immortalized by Degas in *L'Absinthe*. More respectable bourgeois women like Berthe Morisot and Mary Cassatt could not frequent such establishments and complained that they missed out on important technical and intellectual discussions, as well as the fun and

Édouard Manet, *At the Café*, 1874
Boston, Museum of Fine Arts

This, one of Manet's first representations of café life, recreates the atmosphere of the Thursday night meetings at the café in the late 1860s. Here avant-garde artists—including Manet, Degas, Monet, and Renoir—met to talk, drink, and argue about the nature of modern art.

**Around 1875 the Nouvelle-Athènes
on the Place Pigalle in Montmartre
took over from the Café Guerbois
as the regular meeting place for
Impressionist artists and their
friends, journalists, writers, actors,
models, and aesthetes.**

G. C. A., Paris

794 Montmartre. — La rue Pigalle — Nouvelle Athènes.

CAFÉ TORTONI.

35

**The Café Tortoni, situated on the boulevard des Ital-
iens, was a favorite haunt of elegant boulevardiers
such as Manet. During the 1870s it was too smart
(and too expensive) for the likes of Monet and
Renoir, who preferred the Guerbois and the
Nouvelle-Athènes.**

Jean-François Raffaeli, *Bohemians at the Café*, c. 1885
Bordeaux, Musée des Beaux-Arts

Although he took part in the Impressionist exhibitions of
1880 and 1881, Raffaeli was more of a Realist than an
Impressionist artist. The closed-off background across
most of the painting forces our attention on the figures
and contrasts with the vignette of trees and pedestrians
on the right of the street.

the heated arguments. Often these arguments were initiated by Degas,
who (according to Caillebotte) "has introduced disunity into our midst
and spends all his time haranguing everybody in the Nouvelle-Athènes."
The get-togethers, exchanges, and personalities were vividly described
by the Anglo-Irish novelist George Moore, who was living in Paris at the
time. Moore described not only the artists that he admired—particularly
Degas and Manet—but also the lively and sometimes violent discussions
that took place, one of which resulted in a duel between Manet and the
critic Duranty in the forest of Saint-Germain (Zola was Manet's second).
Having resolved their differences, the two men returned that evening to
the Guerbois—apparently the best of friends. Moore admired Manet
most of all: "Though by birth and by education essentially Parisian, there
was something in his appearance and manner of speaking that often
suggested an Englishman. Perhaps it was his dress—his clean-cut clothes
and figure. That figure! Those square shoulders that swaggered as he

went across the room, and the thin waist . . . would evoke an idea of beauty of line united to that of intellectual expression."[7]

Moore was of course describing a *flâneur:* one whose studied and cultivated air of detachment and exquisite refinement of dress and behavior disguise great sensitivity and acuity of vision. Baudelaire, Degas, Edmund de Goncourt, and Caillebotte all qualified as flâneurs. For Manet, this combination of sharpness, sensitivity, and detachment was all important in his representations of modern life. The artist-flâneur was devoted to promenading the streets and frequenting the cafés. Here over a coffee or an aperitif he could survey the passing parade. It was from this perspective that Manet and Degas represented modern life, so that the inhabitants of the cafés and indeed the cafés themselves became the players and the stage for a contemporary reenactment of the "theatre of the streets." The sense of the crowd and of constant street life was due to the rapid growth of Paris in the late nineteenth century. Not only did Paris have a high proportion of single men and women, but by 1891 only

□

Édouard Manet, *George Moore au Café (George Moore at the Nouvelle-Athènes)*, 1879
New York, Metropolitan Museum of Art

Manet painted three portraits of George Moore, an Irish novelist and chronicler of the Impressionists who arrived in Paris in 1873 to study painting and soon became an habitué of the Nouvelle-Athènes. In 1906 he recorded his experiences in *Reminiscences of the Impressionist Painters.*

thirty-two percent of the population had been born in the city, suggesting that the traditional family was no longer central to Parisian life.

Both Manet and Degas focused on the different kinds of working women who frequented these public arenas. In Manet's paintings there is a subtlety and psychological analysis missing from the work of other avant-garde painters, such as Renoir, who painted jolly, relaxed social occasions. The female clientele represented in Manet's cafés and restaurants range from the respectable woman in *Chez le père Lathuille* to the woman in *The Waitress* and the barmaid in *Bar at the Folies-Bergère*, and although Manet frequently used models, they represent the kinds of women he would have come into contact with as a fashionable boulevardier. He painted not only the independent working women who could walk unescorted through the streets of Paris, such as actresses, models, teachers, shop assistants, and laundresses, but also women whose sexual

**Édouard Manet, *Chez le père Lathuille*, 1879
Tournai, Musée des Beaux-Arts**

Here Manet communicates the atmosphere of this well-known outdoor restaurant and its potential as a place for amorous encounters. The woman has finished her meal and may be tempted by the flirtatious advances of the young bohemian (modeled by Louis Gauthier-Lathuille, the son of the proprietor).

favors could be bought. These ranged from streetwalkers to the *grues* (high-class prostitutes). His model for *Nana*, inspired by Zola's novel of the same name, was Henriette Hauser, a popular boulevard figure. He made a number of studies of the infamous Marie Colombier, a demi-mondaine who in the 1860s was known as "le plat du jour." (She was later literally horsewhipped by Sarah Bernhardt, apparently in retaliation for slander.)

Manet frequently used models for these paintings. In *Chez le père Lathuille* first the actress Ellen Andrée and then Judith French, a cousin of Offenbach's, posed for him. The model for the man was Louis Gauthier-Lathuille, the son of the proprietor. Chez le père Lathuille was a well-known restaurant near the Café Guerbois. Manet situates us in the garden where the well-dressed woman is just finishing her meal—eating her fruit on the plate before her, accompanied by a glass of white wine. In the background a waiter stands, poised with a coffeepot—since she is the last customer in the restaurant. Opportuning the woman is a man (either a young artist or a fashionable bohemian) who has clearly not taken part in the meal. He does not even have a chair to sit on and the table is laid for one person. The outcome of the encounter is left unresolved. She may or may not succumb to his advances. The plein air effect achieved by the fresh coloring and loose handling of paint is highly appropriate for evoking the atmosphere of the restaurant's terrace garden.

Manet's re-creation of the smells and ambience of these outdoor restaurants (by then so much a part of pleasurable Parisian life) was greatly admired at the time. When the artist and illustrator George Jeanniot saw the painting in Manet's studio in January 1882, he thought it summed up the delights of Paris: "White cloths, cool greenery, sparkling glasses, light air, delicate smells, all qualities that give these places in Paris a quintessence that the provincial or foreigner senses with delight before he becomes accustomed to them. These pleasures, which each address themselves to a sense and which together ravish all of them simultaneously, form a large part of the attraction of this exquisite town. Before *Chez le père Lathuille* I had a sort of retrospective shock at everything Paris had enabled me to sample by way of agreeable surprises and choice delights."

In *The Waitress*, the focus is as much on the waitress as on the clientele, and we are shown a different kind of establishment: the brasserie Reichshoffen in the boulevard Rochechouart. At this time brasseries were becoming increasingly popular as establishments that sold beer. Before the Revolution of 1848, beer was not commonly drunk in Paris due to its association with peasants and provincial life. During the Second Empire the increasing number of travelers to Paris brought with them their taste for beer.

Apparently Manet admired the waitress and asked her to sit for him. She agreed on the condition that her boyfriend could accompany her to the artist's studio (he is the man in the blue worker's smock in the foreground). Women waiters became more common during the Second Empire, café proprietors having discovered that women assistants increased the sale of drinks. The status of these women could be ambiguous, and nowhere is this more clearly evidenced than in Manet's last great painting, the *Bar at the Folies-Bergère,* where we are presented with yet another kind of establishment dedicated to entertainment and refreshment.

The Folies-Bergère near the rue Bergère took part of its name from the eighteenth-century *folie,* an open-air entertainment area where Parisians could drink and dance. By the 1880s the Folies-Bergère was a fashionable venue: a more upmarket version of the café-concert with both an indoor and an outdoor area with bars, tables, and room for walking about (a *promenoir*) as well as a stage for the "spectacle," that included circuses, acrobats, whole operettas, and ballets. The proprietor Léon Sari charged admission for the entertainment and the drinks cost much more than at cafés. It was therefore an expensive night out and was dominated by wealthier Parisians, including many of Manet's friends: writers, artists, collectors, critics, and members of the Jockey Club.

Manet painted the *Bar at the Folies-Bergère* in his studio (after making preliminary sketches in the Folies-Bergère), where he recreated the bar in the foreground. The painting is set in one of the inside bars, with the smartly dressed waitress, Suzon, gazing seriously at the viewer. Her remote, self-involved look comes as a surprise, given her occupation and glittering surroundings, reflected in the mirror behind her. More astonishing and disturbing, however, is that in the displaced reflection, the woman is leaning toward the male customer, an action that implies a relationship. The reflection casts a shadow over the painting, both literally and figuratively. Visually there is a contrast between the slight blurring of the reflection showing the "compliant woman" and the brilliant array of drinks, fruit, and glassware on the table: the liqueurs, beer, and champagne lined up for the modish clientele, which elements in themselves constitute a tour de force of still life painting. The bottles and fruit on the bar may be a metaphor for sexual exchange. They are certainly commodities—is the girl? Once again Manet has simply posed the ques-

□

Édouard Manet, *The Waitress,* 1879
London, National Gallery

In this scene, which probably takes place in the Brasserie Reichshoffen, Manet has focused on the waitress and blue-smocked worker in the foreground. Our attention is drawn to this area because of the vivacity of the paint work (particularly in the handling of the glasses of beer) and the deeper space. There are deliberate spatial ambiguities in this painting, perhaps best summed up by the troubling effect of the bowler hat in the middleground and the flatness of the decorative panel of the dancer, which acts as a backdrop rather than as a background to the work.

tion, forcing the viewer to look closely at the work and consider its
implications.

The champagne bottles on display and drunk in quantities at the Folies-
Bergère are a far cry from the representation of absinthe addiction in
Degas's painting *Absinthe*, for which Montmartre (specifically, the
Nouvelle-Athènes) provided the setting. Absinthe—or the "green muse,"
as the poets called it—was a liqueur made from wormwood and was first
manufactured commercially by H. L. Pernod in 1797. It was a popular
working-class drink by the beginning of the nineteenth century and was
increasingly drunk during the Second Empire. By the end of the century

43

Édouard Manet, *Bar at the Folies-Bergère*, 1881–1882
London, Home House Trustees, Courtauld Institute
Galleries

Page 42: detail

Manet recreates the brilliant new entertainments at
the Folies-Bergère—a spectacular kind of café-concert
that included an outdoor area as well as the indoor
area that we see here. Along the bar counter in the
foreground are an impressive array of bottles: champagne, Bass pale ale (with the red triangle), and
crème de menthe. These, together with the background's shimmering reflection of elegant men of the
world and well-known demimondaines (such as Méry
Laurent, the woman with the yellow gloves), contrast
with the detached and slightly withdrawn expression
on the face of the bar girl, Suzon.

its consumption by volume exceed that of all liquors combined. It was nearly seventy percent alcohol. No wonder, then, that the writer and art critic Alfred Delvau thought it "a terrible and frightening drink in which you lose your footing right away and head for infinity."[8]

Degas's couple are absorbed in their own thoughts: the woman with her glass of absinthe, the man drinking a *mazagran* (iced black coffee), a hangover cure. The coloring is restricted and subdued, withheld so that the viewer does not become emotionally involved with the work. This detachment extends to the way in which the artist has portrayed the two protagonists: physically close but psychologically cut off from each other, the woman barely conscious of the external world (and perhaps waiting for the effect of the drink to plunge her into infinity), the man smoking and looking away into the distance. The viewer is physically close to the two (presumably our vantage point is at the adjacent table in the foreground and facing the couple) but again psychologically distanced by their lack of communication and by the marble tables that act as a "floating" barrier (the tables have no legs). The painting exposes the wretchedness of poverty and alcoholism.

Edgar Degas, *Femmes à la terrasse d'un café*, 1877
Paris, Musée du Louvre, Cabinet des Dessins

This scene takes place at night in a café terrace on the boulevard Montmartre. In front of us are depicted four prostitutes in various attitudes of lassitude and boredom as they wait for clients. Once again Degas has distanced us physically, psychologically, and emotionally from the women by the blocking devices in the foreground: the chair and the café columns, as well as the women's facial expressions.

In the 1870s Degas also made numerous pastels and prints of the women
performers at the café-concerts. He preferred the Café des Ambassadeurs and sought out and drew two of its stars, Emma Valadon and
Amélie Bécat, whose performances he described as being a mixture of
the delicate and the gross. Certainly, he portrays these women (and their
knowing sexual exchanges with the crowd) in this way. The same could
be said of Degas's prostitutes marking time and waiting for clients in
Femmes à la terrasse d'un café. The scene here takes place in a café on the
boulevard Montmartre at night. The women are shown in the glassed-in
terrace of a café, the roof supports dividing the composition arbitrarily
and giving it a sense of staccato movement. Beyond are the gaslit
shops of the grand boulevards. The women are sitting at their marble-
topped tables looking bored—there are no clients tonight. Degas has

45

37 - PARIS - Entrée des jardins
du Moulin de la Galette

46

given them the same brutish features to emphasize their degradation. Because Montmartre was a place largely devoted to entertainment and inhabited by shop assistants, artisans, and tradespeople, it was, as we have seen, ideally situated to provide the Impressionists with modern subject matter. It also provided the perfect milieu for them to get together and exhibit their works. Renoir felt completely at home there and complained that he felt "lost" when he was away from Montmartre. In 1875 he rented a house on the rue Cortot not far from the Moulin de la Galette, recently converted into a café restaurant where dances were held on Sunday afternoons. In the 1880s an art gallery was established at 19 boulevard Montmartre with Theo van Gogh in charge. Vincent van Gogh was living with Theo in Montmartre from 1886 at 54 rue Lepic. He exhibited his work in restaurants along the boulevard de Clichy and occasionally sold paintings in exchange for meals or money to buy paints. As well as painting the cafés, restaurants, and fruit and vegetable shops that filled the pavements of the area, he was one of the few artists to paint views of the suburban landscape with its quarries, windmills, and gardens, although he did not take part in the meetings at the Nouvelles-Athènes. If Impressionism was conceived in a café, it was in a more literal sense "made" on the banks of the Seine and at Barbizon and Fontainebleau. One of the many discussions in the Café Guerbois had concerned the efficacy of painting in the open air and the use of shadows. Outside Paris, along the banks of the Seine and in the forest of Fontainebleau, Monet, Renoir, Bazille, Pissarro, Morisot, and Sisley had worked at the "new" art. They focused on suburban leisure and pleasure areas that were generally popular at the time, particularly for Parisians: at Asnières, Argenteuil, Bougival, Chatou, Marly, and Louveciennes, which were all served by the railway from the Gare Saint-Lazare.

Monet's first large-scale painting was the *Le Déjeuner sur l'herbe*, painted while he was staying at the Hôtel du Lion d'Or at Chailly with Camille Doncieux, his future wife. It was never finished and the artist later cut the painting into pieces, of which the central panel is the largest surviving fragment. He appears to have been competing with Manet's painting of the same name exhibited two years earlier. Monet recast it in a more modern idiom in the open air and successfully recreated the type of picnic enjoyed by the middle classes at the time. Monet preferred a more naturalistic rendition of bourgeois recreation, and this is particularly evident in the detailed painting of the food spread out for the picnic. There is a sense of relaxation inherent in the airiness and casual attitudes of the party.

At this time picnicking and eating outdoors in general became more widespread. Parisians taking their lunches to the park, racetrack, or suburban attraction were conducting their own version of the picnics and hunt breakfasts that had formed an enjoyable part of aristocratic recreation before the revolution and were now being appropriated by the middle classes. Daytrippers who forgot to bring along the appropriate hamper could buy food and drink from cafés and small food stands. Further out of Paris there were facilities for hiring a hamper and servant—as Monet's picnickers appear to have done (this is clear in the large sketch for the composition now in Moscow). In *An Impressionist Picnic* Manzana Pissarro has left us with a vivid record of an Impressionist picnic in which his father and friends (including Gauguin and Cézanne) are depicted painting, eating, and talking out of doors against an industrial background while Madame Cézanne busily cooks a meal over a fire. In 1869 both Monet and Renoir painted at La Grenouillière (literally "the froggery") a popular swimming area for Parisians and one especially favored by artists and writers. Situated not far from Bougival at Croissy island, its facilities included a restaurant, cafés-concerts, and balls, with

Guillaumin, Pissarro, Gauguin, Cézanne. Dame Cézanne, le petit manzana.   manzana · Pissarro

48

Manzana Pissarro,
An Impressionistic Picnic, 1881
Menton, collection of Félix Pissarro

Here Manzana Pissarro has vividly captured the sense of a day's outing away from the grime of industrialization evident in the chimneys of the Pontoise gasworks visible in the background. In the center (from left) Guillaumin, Pissarro, and Gauguin are waiting for lunch cooked by Madame Cézanne. This process is being carefully watched by a presumably ravenous Manzana, while Cézanne continues hard at work on his landscape.

boats and swimsuits for hire, plus food and drink sold on the riverbanks for alfresco refreshment—all designed to prove irresistible to Parisian visitors. By 1870 tourism had taken over these outlying districts of Paris and was in full swing, a state of affairs commented on by contemporary writers who loathed the crowds and the picnic debris and lamented the passing of rustic tranquillity. Presumably Monet and Renoir hoped that the subject's epicurean associations would reconcile their audience to the unorthodox handling of the subject.

50

Pierre Auguste Renoir, *La Grenouillère*, 1869
Stockholm, Nationalmuseum

Monet painted a similar view of the "Camembert," the round jetty on which people gathered to relax and chat, with glimpses of swimmers to the left. In his concern to record momentary sensations of color and light, Renoir has opted for light colors and varied brushwork: a broad square brush has been used to make stabbing horizontal strokes in the foreground, and a smaller pointed brush to dot the leaves on the tree in the center. The more blended strokes beyond evoke a summery haze of foliage.

Suburban and rural cafés, restaurants, and inns provided the artists with modern subject matter not only at La Grenouillière but at many of the other pleasure domes as well. Renoir painted himself and friends in *Le Cabaret de la Mère Anthony*. An old-fashioned auberge well liked by artists and bohemians, Mère Anthony's was situated near Fontainebleau at Marlotte. Renoir was later to describe it as "a real village inn." In the painting he included himself and Sisley sitting at the table while a servant cleared the remains of their meal. The realist treatment of the painting was

Vincent van Gogh, *Le Restaurant de la Sirène à Asnières*, 1887
Paris, Musée d'Orsay

In the year or so before he went to the south of France, van Gogh began eliminating darker tones from his palette and experimenting with high-keyed color combinations, as evident in this painting of the Sirène restaurant on the outskirts of Paris at Joinville-le-Pont.

Pierre-Auguste Renoir, *Le Cabaret de la mère Anthony*, 1886
Stockholm, Nationalmuseum

Here Renoir has portrayed the plain old-fashioned inn at Marlotte on the edge of the Fontainebleau forest in an appropriately realist fashion. The bold brush strokes and dark tonalities are more reminiscent of Courbet than the Impressionists. The inn had been the haunt of bohemian artists and writers who over the years had contributed to the wall decoration in the background. Renoir has included (from left) himself, the painter Jacques Le Coeur, and Sisley seated around the table with the eponymous Mère Anthony in the background.

appropriate because, by all accounts, Mère Anthony's guests were riotous. The Goncourts visiting in 1863 had been shocked by "Anthony, who harbors wretched painters, along with Murger's disgraceful phalanstery and licensed harem."[9]

Renoir set *Le Déjeuner des canotiers* (*Luncheon of the Boating Party*) on the terrace of the restaurant Fournaise at Chatou, overlooking the Seine. The models for this convivial and relaxed gathering—here shown drinking and talking at the end of the meal—were mainly Renoir's friends and acquaintances, including the restaurant proprietor's son, Alphonse Fournaise. The composition, coloring, and handling of the work are in marked contrast to *Le Cabaret de la Mère Anthony*.

In their later years, many of the Impressionists settled outside Paris: Monet at Giverny in 1883, Renoir in the south of France at the end of the century, and Pissarro in Eragny in 1888. Their visits to the Nouvelle-Athènes and Café Guerbois became infrequent. In the early 1890s Pissarro, Sisley, Renoir, and Caillebotte met regularly (on the first Thursday of each month) for dinner at the Café Riche on the boulevard des Italiens, their growing success and financial security having earned them the privilege of dining in more expensive restaurants. Madame Hoschedé recalled her trips to Paris with Monet, when they would base themselves at the Hôtel Terminus and spend their days indulging their delight in art and good food. As well as the Café Riche, they would visit restaurants renowned for their cuisine: Prunier's, Drouant, the Café de Paris, and the Café Anglais. It is tempting to speculate whether over these increasingly costly and sophisticated meals the Impressionists missed the early heady days of cheaper wine and their disputes, duels, and passionate discussions about modern art.

Pages 54-55
Pierre-Auguste Renoir, *Le Déjeuner des canotiers*
(*Luncheon of the Boating Party*), 1880–1881 (detail)
Washington, The Phillips Collection

The end of a langorous summer lunch on the terrace of the restaurant Fournaise is emphasized here by attracting the viewer's attention to the richness of the still life detail reflecting the light. Around them are grouped various friends and acquaintances of the artist, chief among them on the left Aline Charigot, Renoir's future wife. Leaning against the railing is Alphonse Fournaise, the son of the proprietor, while opposite him in the striped smock is the journalist Maggiolo.

Clamart Andouillettes

An andouillette is a small sausage made of pork tripe.

Serves 6
- 6 andouillettes
- 1 onion chopped
- $\frac{1}{2}$ cup white wine
- 6 lettuce hearts
- $\frac{1}{4}$ cup butter
- 1 tablespoon oil
- 3 cups fresh shelled green peas
- 1 bouquet garni
- 1 teaspoon sugar
- 2 tablespoons crème fraîche or whipping cream
- Nutmeg

Place the andouillettes in an ovenproof dish, cover with the chopped onion and white wine, and bake in 350° oven.

Blanch the lettuce hearts in boiling water, cool in cold water, and drain. Cook slowly in the oil and butter until tender but not brown, then cover and braise.

Place the green peas in a pot with a small amount of water, the bouquet garni, and the sugar. Cover and steam 15 minutes, then uncover and let the water evaporate. Purée through the large-hole disk of a food mill, then blend with the cream and season with nutmeg. Arrange the cooked andouillettes in a serving dish and surround with the lettuce hearts and the pea purée.

Pâté en Croûte

Serves 8 to 10

For the stuffing:
- $\frac{1}{2}$ lb. veal fillet or round
- $\frac{1}{2}$ lb. pork loin
- $\frac{1}{2}$ lb. ham
- $\frac{1}{2}$ lb. sweet sausage stuffing
- $\frac{1}{2}$ lb. thin bacon strips
- 1 tablespoon salt
- Pepper
- $\frac{1}{2}$ cup Madeira wine
- Fines herbes
- 1 shallot, chopped
- 1 dozen pistachios or
- 1 small truffle, thinly sliced

For the crust:
- 5 cups flour
- 2 cups butter
- $\frac{1}{2}$ cup water, to which has been added 1 teaspoon salt
- 1 egg to coat the crust

Slice all the meats (except the bacon) into small thin strips and sprinkle with salt and pepper. Pour the Madeira over the meat, then sprinkle with the fines herbes and chopped shallot. Mix well so that the meat absorbs the flavors. Marinate 5 to 6 hours.

Prepare the crust by lightly mixing the flour with the softened butter and moistening with the salted water. Shape the dough into a ball, flatten, then shape and flatten again. Repeat this procedure three times, then wrap the dough in a cloth and leave it in a cool place. Butter a pâté mold and line it with three-fourths of the dough, leaving a 3-inch overhang. Line the bottom with the bacon strips and cover with a thin layer of sausage stuffing. Continue making layers, alternating the different meats and filling in the gaps with the sausage stuffing. On top of the pâté, arrange the pistachios or the truffle slices. Trim away the excess dough, and cover the pâté with the remaining dough. With a rolled piece of brown paper or foil, make a little "chimney" and insert it into the dough to let the cooking vapor escape. Brush the dough with the egg yolk. Bake in 350 degree oven $1\frac{1}{2}$ hours. Allow pâté to cool before unmolding.

Parisian Vegetable Soup

This is one of many variations on the famous Vichyssoise.

Serves 6
- 6 leek whites
- 6 or 7 medium potatoes
- 1 bunch chopped parsley
- 3 tablespoons butter
- 1 tablespoon oil
- 2 quarts water
- 2 tablespoons crème fraîche or whipping cream
- Salt and pepper

To prepare the vegetables:
Carefully clean the leeks. Quarter them lengthwise, then slice. Peel and dice the potatoes, and chop the parsley.

To make the soup:
Melt the butter with the oil in a heavy casserole. Add the leeks and the parsley. Cook slowly.
Just before the leeks brown, pour in the water and bring to a boil. Drop the diced potatoes into the boiling water and cook about 40 minutes. When the soup is done, pour it into a tureen, add the cream, and season to taste. Sprinkle with more minced parsley before serving.

Loing Bream

The Loing is a little river near Paris.

Serves 4
- 4 medium bream

For the marinade:
- 1 cup olive oil
- 1 lemon cut into slices
- Thyme, bay leaves

For the sauce:
- $\frac{1}{2}$ cup white wine
- 2 minced shallots
- 2 egg yolks
- $\frac{1}{2}$ cup butter
- Chopped parsley
- Salt and pepper

The quantities given are for 4 people. Adjust the recipe as needed, allowing about $\frac{1}{2}$ lb. of fish per person.

Scale and clean the fish, then wash them carefully and soak in fresh water.

Rinse and drain, then marinate in the oil with the lemon, thyme, and bay leaves about 20 minutes. Preheat the grill.

Meanwhile, slowly cook the shallots in $\frac{1}{2}$ cup of white wine, cooking until the liquid is reduced to 1 spoonful. Remove from heat and allow to cool, then beat the egg yolks into the mixture.

Transfer the sauce to a double boiler over low heat, and gradually stir in the butter and parsley. Season with salt and pepper and keep warm in the double boiler while you cook the bream.

Cook the bream on a hot grill, season, and serve with the sauce.

Bream is hard to find in fish markets. Carp makes a nice substitute.

Vegetables with Mayonnaise

The vegetables:
- 1 cauliflower cut into florets
- Carrot sticks
- Lettuce hearts
- Small purple artichokes
- Cherry tomatoes

The mayonnaise:
- 2 egg yolks
- 1 teaspoon mustard
- Salt and pepper
- Olive oil
- Lemon juice

Beat together the egg yolks and mustard in a big bowl. Add the salt and pepper, then gradually add the olive oil in a thin stream while beating vigorously with a wooden spoon.

When the mayonnaise is firm enough, carefully add a few drops of lemon juice (too much will liquefy the mayonnaise).

Serve with the raw vegetables.

Chicken Casserole "Père Lathuille"

Serves 4
- 2 small young chickens
- $\frac{3}{4}$ lb. each of the following vegetables:
- minced carrots
- minced turnips
- potatoes (cut into balls with a melon baller from large, very firm potatoes)
- quartered artichoke hearts
- minced onions
- 1 cup chicken stock
- Salt and pepper

Blanch all vegetables (except the onions) in boiling water for 5 minutes.

Lightly brown the chickens in an earthenware casserole. Add the vegetables, then pour in the chicken stock. Season with salt and pepper, cover, and simmer on very low heat about 50 minutes.

Sauté the minced onions and add them to the pot.

Serve in the cooking casserole.

Asparagus with Mousseline Sauce

"Françoise, had you come five minutes earlier, you would have seen Madame Imbert pass by, carrying asparagus twice the size of Madame Callot's. Try to find out from her maid where she got them. Since you've been serving us asparagus in all possible ways this year, you could have gotten such nice ones for our visitors."

"It wouldn't surprise me if they came from Monsieur le Curé," said Françoise.

"Ah indeed, that's right, my poor Françoise," answered my aunt, shrugging her shoulders, "from Monsieur le Curé! You well know that he only grows silly little nothings of asparagus. Just like my arm—not yours, of course, but my poor little arm—which became so much thinner this year . . ."

—Marcel Proust, *Remembrance of Things Past*

Serves 4
- 3 lbs. asparagus (the small green ones are tastier)
- $\frac{1}{2}$ lb. (2 sticks) butter
- 3 egg yolks
- 3 tablespoons cold water
- Juice of $\frac{1}{2}$ lemon
- Salt and pepper
- A dash of cayenne pepper
- 3 tablespoons whipped cream

To cook the asparagus:
Peel the asparagus and cook them in salted boiling water about 35 minutes. Drain, then set aside on an asparagus platter.

To make the sauce:
Melt the butter, then allow to cool until lukewarm. Place the egg yolks, cold water, and lemon juice in a heavy-bottom saucepan. Set on low heat and warm very gently (excessive heat will cook the egg yolks and curdle the sauce). Beat vigorously with a wire whisk to a thick, foamy cream, then remove from heat and whisk a few seconds more. Gradually beat in the melted butter as for mayonnaise. Season with salt, pepper, and a dash of cayenne pepper.
Keep warm. Then, just before serving, fold in the whipped cream. Serve in a sauceboat alongside the asparagus.

Crêpes Suzette

Makes about 20 crêpes
- 2 cups flour
- 2 whole eggs and 3 yolks
- $\frac{1}{2}$ teaspoon salt
- 2 cups cold milk
- 2 teaspoons orange flower water
- $\frac{1}{4}$ cup melted butter

To prepare the crêpe batter:
Sift the flour into an earthenware bowl. Make a well in the center and drop in the eggs, yolks, salt, and cold milk. Beat vigorously with a wire whisk until batter is completely smooth, then continue beating while adding the melted butter. Stir in the orange flower water. Allow to rest 2 to 3 hours.

For slightly puffed crêpes, fold in 2 egg whites beaten until firm before cooking.

To cook and serve the crêpes:
- $3\frac{1}{2}$ tablespoons butter
- 4 tablespoons sugar
- 2 tablespoons grated orange rinds
- 1 (1 shotglass) curaçao
- raspberries

Cook the crêpes and keep them warm.

In a bowl, cream the butter and sugar and add the grated orange rind and curaçao.

Spread a small amount of this cream (about one teaspoon per crêpe) on one-half of each crêpe. Fold in half, garnish with a few raspberries, and serve.

Scalloped Potatoes Anna

Serves 6
- 3 lbs. potatoes
- Salt and pepper
- Nutmeg
- $\frac{1}{2}$ lb. (2 sticks) butter

Wash and peel the potatoes, then cut them into $\frac{1}{8}$-inch-thick slices. Dry them thoroughly with a towel. Generously butter a round mold and fill with layers of potato slices seasoned with salt and pepper.

Arrange them overlapping each other, in concentric circles, changing direction for each layer. Sprinkle each layer with grated nutmeg.

Melt the butter, and while it is still hot, pour it over the potatoes. Gently tilt the mold in all directions so that the butter bastes all layers. Bake in 400° oven about 40 minutes, then unmold on a warm serving dish, as for a cake.

Detail from page 71

2

Most of the Impressionists portrayed their home life at some point in their careers, doing so in a variety of ways that often depended

THE HOME

on their own social background and domestic situation. Paintings of family meals vary from the formal, like Paul Signac's *Le Petit Déjeuner* to the more relaxed and modest get-togethers, painted for instance by Marie Bracquemond in *Under the Lamp*. Some, like Monet, focused more closely on family life and the intimate delights of mealtime.

In the domestic sphere the woman reigned supreme. Respectable women were prohibited from venturing into the "dangerous" new public spaces described in Chapter 1. Their excursions were restricted to promenades or drives in the parks (with a male escort). There was also shopping—perhaps to the Place de la Madeleine, where Auguste-Félix Fauchon dealt exclusively in the best French products, including groceries, poul-

64

☐

Claude Monet, *Luncheon*, 1868
Frankfurt, Städelsches Kunstinstitut

Monet's letters of 1868 record his delight in the company of his son Jean (born in 1967), who with his mother was often featured in Monet's paintings of these years. Here Monet communicates the child's liveliness and his impatience to be eating the food on the table, which has been painted carefully.

try, charcuterie, cheese, biscuits, confectionery, wines, and liqueurs. Later he was to open a salon de thé-pâtisserie. In France from around 1770 there were restaurants that ladies could visit with a family party (although in England it was another hundred years before a lady could be seen in a public dining room with propriety). Thus, for middle-class women the home was the center of their lives, where they focused on domestic life and the rituals of eating, drinking, and entertainment.

The woman ran the household and, depending on her situation in life, either supervised or undertook many of the household chores, such as the cooking. Traditional French home cooking consists of recipes handed down from mother to daughter with regional variations. Soups were an integral feature of this cuisine, and until well after the Revolution (and longer in many rural areas) soup was the last meal of the day—the word *soupe* originally referred to the slice of bread onto which the contents of the cooking pot (potage) were poured. French home cooking of this kind

Pierre-Auguste Renoir, *La Fin du déjeuner* (*The End of Lunch*), 1879 (detail)
Frankfurt, Städelsches Kunstinstitut

Renoir has made a careful study here of the glassware and porcelain that signal the end of the meal. The fractional view of the man lighting his cigarette on the right does not prevent him from dominating the composition; the black of his suit serves as an anchor and contrasts with the white tablecloth. Ellen Andrée, who also served as Degas's model for *L'Absinthe*, poses here for the woman holding out her liqueur glass.

made use of freshly picked vegetables from the garden and meats roasted in a variety of ways, as well as cheaper cuts of meat simmered for a long time to produce marmites (stews), ragoûts, and matelotes (see recipes). The pot-au-feu was a favorite. As a dish that was, according to Mirabeau, the "foundation of empires," it provided in one dish a soup (the broth), boiled meat (usually beef), and vegetables. The skimmed broth was served with toasted croutons sprinkled with cheese, then the bone marrow was given to the most venerable member of the household, and finally the sliced meat and vegetables were eaten with various garnishes, according to region. The leftover meat could be eaten hot or cold or even be made into another dish by the thrifty housewife.

In Marie Bracquemond's *Under the Lamp*, this kind of cooking is very much in evidence. Here we have the artist's home at Sèvres, where the Bracquemonds frequently entertained artist friends and are here shown playing host to Alfred Sisley and his wife. On the table is a pile of plates,

Marie Bracquemond, *Under the lamp: Alfred Sisley and His Wife at the Bracquemond Home at Sèvres,* 1887
Private collection

Alfred Sisley and his wife were regular visitors to the Bracquemond home at Sèvres. Madame Sisley is shown here with her back half-turned to the viewer while her husband sits opposite, ready to partake in an informal meal of cuisine grand-mère: a steaming casserole, bread, wine, and dressing for the salad are already laid out on the table.

a loaf of bread, and a steaming bowl of soup. The placement of both the food and the guests is extremely casual, contrasting sharply with the greater formality then obligatory in upper middle-class households.

In the latter part of the nineteenth century, the standard of bourgeois home cooking improved, owing to a number of factors. The solid iron fuel range came into general use in middle-class homes in the 1860s, with gas appearing some twenty years later. This revolution in equipment meant that cooking need not be done over an open fire or in a coal-fired brick oven. Sautés, sauces, and soufflés were within the means of any middle-class household possessing one of these new ovens, which had made cooking a more enjoyable activity.

The publication of cookbooks that proliferated at this time also improved the standard of cooking at home. For the middle classes who wanted their tables to reflect their status, traditional family recipes were not always adequate. Cookbooks not only extended their repertoire (and gave them ideas about what to cook and how to cook it) but also informed them on matters of etiquette.

Two of the most influential cookbooks in the late nineteenth century were Monsieur A. Viard's *Le Cuisinier impérial*, first published in 1806 and reprinted throughout the century under a title that changed to *royal* or *national*, depending on the current regime. Viard's book presented problems for the domestic cook because the recipes were frequently too ambitious or merely impractical. *La Cuisinière de la campagne et de la ville, ou Nouvelle Cuisine économique* by Louis Eustache Audot was first published in 1818 and by 1901 was in its seventy-ninth edition. In the introduction to the forty-eighth edition in 1868, Audot emphasized that this cookbook was primarily practical and popular and aimed at the middle-class household. He heaped scorn on other well-known writers who exhorted the domestic chef to ever-increasing extravagances in the making of sauces and bouillon, such as the famous injunction in Viard's *Le Cuisinier impérial* to *"rôtir vert douze canards afin d'en tirer le jus pour accomoder quinze oeufs"* ("roast twelve ducks to get the sauce for fifteen eggs").

Audot's recipes included not only retested recipes from (in his words) "good old *Cuisinière bourgeoise,*" but also recipes designed for more sophisticated tastes: soufflés, pastries, sauces, and so forth, plus more exotic recipes from foreign countries. The book is also clearly intended to instruct and inform. He gives, for instance, every conceivable method for cooking poultry, game, fish, and red meat, which can be grilled, baked, steamed, roasted, sautéed, and then served with any number of

□

**Claude Monet, *Still Life with a Pheasant*,
c. 1861 (detail)
Rouen, Musée des Beaux-Arts**

**The inclusion of game was rare in Monet's still lifes,
although game was an important category in
seventeenth-century Flemish still life painting. Here
Monet delights in the rich colors of the bird's
plumage.**

sauces, most of them relatively straightforward in preparation. Clarity and variety are the order of the day.

In his long introduction he includes practical advice on buying kitchen equipment and the latest design in ovens (with illustrations), as well as instructions regarding food presentation and decoration. He advises the socially conscious hostess on the number of courses she should serve when entertaining at lunchtime: First the entrée, consisting of soup and hors d'oeuvre, followed by several plates of meat, game, poultry, and fish, together with sauces, ragoûts, and purées, the quantity determined by the number of people at the table. Next the entremets, both sweet and savory (it was not uncommon then to serve sweet and savory dishes at the same time). This could consist of egg, vegetable, and fish dishes as well as crèmes (creams and custards) and pastries. The final dessert course would include lighter sweet dishes and fruit dishes, such as Poires à la Bourdaloue (see recipe), a dessert created by a pastry chef whose establishment was on the rue Bourdaloue in Paris. It consists of halved William pears that are poached and then immersed in vanilla-flavored frangipane. They are then covered with crushed macaroons and baked in the oven. Finally, Audot dictated the table placement and precise placement of dishes for a luncheon or dinner party, again with detailed illustrations. *Nouvelle Cuisine économique* was clearly aimed at both the metropolitan and provincial bourgeoisie with social aspirations. The lady of the house could use it as a guide in directing her cook and other servants.

Berthe Morisot's *In the Dining Room,* for instance, reminds us of the artist's own social position as an upper middle-class woman with a household to supervise. She regularly entertained Monet, Caillebotte, and Pissarro, as well as writers such as Mallarmé and Zola. In her paintings, Morisot depicted every aspect of her domestic life, including her servants going about their daily chores—possibly in accordance with the strictures laid down by the irrepressible Audot. The servant in this painting is shown in the dining room apparently in the process of mixing a sauce or dressing.

Occasionally the Impressionists focused on the etiquette of meals at home. Caillebotte, who came from a wealthy and haut-bourgeois background suggested constraint and claustrophobia in *Le Déjeuner* where his mother and brother are shown lunching in a heavily curtained dark room. The unobtrusive servant, the family silver and glassware carefully laid out, and the eaters spaced some feet apart (making conversation difficult) contribute to the oppressive atmosphere. Paul Signac, who also

Berthe Morisot,
In the Dining Room, 1886
Washington, National Gallery of
Art

In 1881 Morisot and her husband
bought land on the rue de Villejust
in Passy near the Bois de Boulogne.
They moved into their newly built
house in 1883. The house and
garden became the setting for a
number of subjects in which she
recorded her domestic life with her
husband and daughter Julie, as well
as painting the servants going about
their daily chores—as in this
painting.

Gustave Caillebotte, *Le Déjeuner*, 1876
Paris, private collection

Caillebotte has emphasized the formality and
claustrophobia of upper middle-class mealtimes—in
this instance his own family, since he shows his
mother and brother dining, waited on by their
servant René. The sense of constraint comes not only
from the pervading gloom and ponderous

furnishings, but also from the way in which the artist
has manipulated space so that the viewer is distanced
from the diners by the (exaggerated) expanse of the
table and the plates and glassware, while the diners
are similarly distanced from each other.

came from a well-to-do background, recreated an atmosphere of stiffness and formality in *Le Petit Déjeuner*. Here the large expanse of white tablecloth between the two primary figures emphasizes their lack of communication (added to which neither is looking at the other), and the erect profile of the servant acts as a further barrier. One has, too, the impression of a formal placement governing the arrangement of the objects on the table.

□

Paul Signac, *Le Petit Déjeuner*, 1886–1887
Otterlo, Rijksmuseum Kröller-Müller

Signac's use of strict profiles and a frontal view, together with the careful placement of forms on the table and the strong *contrejour* or back light, all give this painting a stiff artificiality and stress the formality and restraint that accompanied bourgeois mealtimes.

The introduction of the midday *déjeuner* dated from the 1789 revolution (until then the midday meal was called *dîner*), with the evening meal taking place at the end of the afternoon. Sunday luncheon was a symbol of family life, with the best silver, porcelain, and glass on display. Between courses the guests might take a turn about the garden or even indulge in a game of lawn bowling. The family lunch portrayed by Louise Abbéma in *Luncheon in the Conservatory* is a slightly more informal affair, owing to the naturalistic treatment of some of the details and the inclusion of the little girl—gazing upon the food—and the dog. The erect posture of the older woman on the left reminds us of the etiquette attached to such occasions. From the middle of the nineteenth century, treatises on etiquette multiplied. At this time also polite people stopped eating chicken with their fingers or mixing the salad with their hands, and tableware in middle-class households would include such refinements as cutlet holders and knife rests. Mary Cassatt confessed to being shocked by Cézanne's provincial table manners when she met him at Giverny in 1894: he apparently scraped his soup plate, ate with his knife (which he never put down during the meal), and even took his steak in his fingers and pulled the meat off the bone.

Louise Abbéma,
Luncheon in the Conservatory, 1877
Pau, Musée des Beaux-Arts

Abbéma's photographic realism exemplified in this painting was ideally suited to the portrayal of this lunchtime scene in the conservatory of an upper middle-class home.

Claude Monet, *Dîner chez Sisley*
(*The Artist's Family at Dinner*), 1867
Zurich, collection of E. G. Bührle

Here Monet has painted an
ordinary family dinner. The only
light comes from the gas lamp over
the table and from the log fire. He
has included himself in the
painting (facing the viewer) with
Camille and his son Jean. In the
background gloom a servant waits,
ready to take the plates.

By contrast Claude Monet's many paintings of family life with Camille
Doncieux and their son Jean (born in 1867), produced in the years
leading up to the first Impressionist exhibition of 1874, are relaxed
sunny scenes completely devoid of the restraint that was such a feature
of upper middle-class life. This is perhaps not surprising, given Monet's
petit bourgeois background (he was the son of a grocer) and the fact that
he and Camille did not marry until 1870. In a letter to Bazille he de-
scribes the happiness of family life in spite of pressing financial worries:
"After dinner, dear friend, I find in my cottage a good fire and a won-
derful little family. If only you could see how cute your little godson is
now! This little creature absolutely fascinates me, and believe me, dear
friend, I am glad to have him."[10]

In *Dîner Chez Sisley (The Artist's Family at Dinner)*, Monet included himself
dining with Camille and little Jean in a high chair with a maid in atten-
dance in the background ready to take the soup plates and bring on
the next course. There is a poignancy in the way in which Monet has

captured the intimacy of this family ritual where traditional French home cooking is being sampled. In *Luncheon* the whole scene is enlivened by Jean's impatience to be eating. He drums his spoon in anticipation; a discarded toy lies under the chair on the left. The sense of casualness and of the fleeting moment is enhanced by the empty chairs in the foreground, one of which belongs to the artist who is keeping the family waiting. Lunch is simple: boiled eggs, steak and fried potatoes, salad, and bread, followed by fruit—all laid out on the table ready for Monet who, ironically, insisted on punctuality at mealtimes.

The rituals of daily life at home are vividly portrayed by the women artists who showed their works at the Impressionist exhibitions: Berthe Morisot, Marie Bracquemond, and the American Mary Cassatt. As respectable women none of them could spend time in the most obvious modern venues. Their solution was to paint modern subjects that were accessible to them at home and in the public spaces that they could frequent, and not to allow such restrictions to prevent them from experimenting with new and avant-garde techniques. Some, like Mary Cassatt, endowed these subjects with a probity and a seriousness rarely attached to such subjects.

Cassatt's *Five O'Clock Tea* depicts polite entertainment: the artist's sister Lydia is having tea with an elegantly dressed friend. Cassatt herself came from a wealthy and cultivated background, and here she has recreated a fashionable social activity that would have taken up much of these young ladies' time—calling on friends and acquaintances to take tea.

At this time tea drinking was becoming increasingly popular, and by the turn of the century Parisian ladies were meeting in luxurious tearooms. Tea was frequently served with a dash of cream and small, dry, crispy pastries. At home tea drinking provided an opportunity to show off one's porcelain service and silver, both of which are seen in this painting. There was also an etiquette attached to tea drinking in polite society: for instance, the correct way of holding one's cup or putting down one's spoon, as shown here by Lydia's friend on the right.

Bracquemond's *Teatime* depicts an alfresco setting for the ritual, reminding the viewer that avant-garde women artists could easily experiment with plein air effects in garden settings. *Teatime* entices the viewer by the seductive quality of the coloring and brushwork, but like *Five O'Clock Tea* there is a psychological distance: in this case the woman is preoccupied with her own thoughts and seemingly oblivious to the viewer's interest.

A modish meeting place outside the home, where it was also permissible for ladies to meet, was the *pâtisserie*, or pastry shop. Here they could

consume pastries, tea, coffee, and a glass of wine in stylish surroundings.
One could sample not only pastries but also small cakes such as
madeleines (see recipe), described by Proust as "seashell cakes so strictly
pleated outside and so sensual inside." Jean Béraud's *La Pâtisserie Gloppe*
is a glossy and highly attractive image of the leisure class downing delicious pastries in a spacious and mirrored environment. Such a scene
brings to mind one of the greatest chefs of the nineteenth century:
Marie-Antoine Carême, who was first and foremost a pastry chef. Basing
his baked goods on architectural drawings, he created spectacular effects
in sugar, nougat, marzipan, and meringue. Carême is credited with either inventing or perfecting nougat, large meringues, croquembouche,
vol-au-vent, and puff pastry—all sensuous delights we continue to sample and enjoy today.

Jean Béraud, 1889

Game Pâté with Truffles

Serves 8
- The back and 2 boned hind legs of a large hare
- 6 ounces fat bacon
- 2 diced truffles
- Salt, pepper, and allspice
- $\frac{1}{2}$ cup cognac
- 2 lbs. pâté dough
- $\frac{1}{2}$ lb. stuffing (half sweet sausage stuffing, half ground hare meat, prepared by the butcher)
- 1 strip pork fat

Cut the hare meat and some of the bacon into small thin strips and marinate with some of the truffles, allspice, and cognac 24 hours. Season with salt and pepper. Line a pâté mold with a thin layer of dough. Cover the bottom with a layer of pâté mixture about 1-inch thick, then alternate with layers of bacon, stuffing, and truffles. Top with the strip of pork fat. Cover with the remaining dough. Place a "chimney" in the center. Brush the top with egg yolk. Bake at 350° about 40 minutes. Remove from oven as soon as juice pours out the "chimney."

Salted Pork with Lentils

Serves 4
- 2 lbs. half-salted pork (back, shoulder, leg, or ham knuckle)
- 1 lb. lentils
- Oil or lard
- $\frac{1}{2}$ lb. pork rind
- 6 oz. chunk smoked bacon, diced
- 2 onions: one minced, the other studded with 4 cloves
- 1 clove garlic
- 1 sliced carrot
- Thyme and bay leaves

Soak the pork in cold water 1 hour. Set on low heat and bring to a boil. Keep on a low boil 5 minutes, then drain and rinse. Cover the lentils with cold water and heat in the same manner. Drain and rinse. In a casserole, lightly brown together the pork rind, bacon, minced onion, garlic, and carrot. Add the meat, lentils, clove-studded onion, and some thyme and bay leaves, then cover with cold water. Cover the casserole and simmer 1 hour and 15 minutes, stirring occasionally. Serve hot.

Parisian Calf's Head

Serves 6
- 1 boned and rolled calf's head
- 3 tablespoons flour
- 1 carrot
- 1 bouquet garni
- 1 onion studded with 2 or 3 cloves
- Juice of 1 lemon
- 1 tablespoon coarse salt
- Peppercorns
- 2 hard-boiled eggs, separated
- 1 tablespoon mustard
- Oil and vinegar
- Fines herbes
- 1 shallot
- Gherkins and capers
- Salt and pepper

Flambé the calf's head to eliminate the remaining hairs and put it in a large pot. Cover with cold water, and boil 10 minutes to remove impurities. Drain and tie with string.

Dissolve the flour in 3 quarts of water. Make a broth by adding the carrot, bouquet garni, studded onion, lemon juice, coarse salt, and a few peppercorns.

Immerse the calf's head in the broth and simmer $1\frac{1}{2}$ hours.

Pass the egg yolks through a sieve and mix with the mustard. Add to this paste a little oil and vinegar, stirring with a wooden spatula until you have a smooth, but still thick sauce. Chop the fines herbes, shallot, and egg whites and mix into the sauce. Add the capers, small "cornichons", salt, and pepper.

Drain the calf's head and serve hot whole or sliced on a bed of lettuce or parsley, accompanied by the sauce.

Roast Pork in Aspic

Serves 4 to 6
- $\frac{1}{2}$ lb. pork rind, trimmed of all fat
- 2 pig's feet, split in half
- 2 lbs. beef or veal bones, sawed into $1\frac{1}{2}$-inch pieces
- 1 veal shank
- 4 carrots, 3 leeks, 2 onions, 3 sage leaves, and bay leaves
- 1 loin roast (2 to 3 lbs.)
- 2 cloves garlic, cut into slivers
- Salt and pepper
- 4 sage leaves
- 1 tablespoon lard
- 2 eggs
- 1 gelatin sheet ($\frac{1}{4}$ gelatin envelope)

Two days before: Make the jelly.
Blanch together the pork rind, pig's feet, and bones, starting with cold water and slowly bringing to a boil.

Boil 5 minutes and rinse. Place with the veal shank in a large kettle filled with 2 quarts of cold water and bring to a boil.

Skim off the surface and drop the vegetables into the water. Simmer slowly 4 to 5 hours. Spoon off the fat, drain with a colander, and allow to cool.

The day before: Cook the pork roast.
Insert the garlic slivers in the meat, season with salt and pepper, and wedge sage leaves between the strips of fat and the meat on the top and bottom of the roast.
Melt the lard in a heavy-bottom casserole. Add the roast, cover, and simmer 1 to 1½ hours (30 minutes per pound). When done, allow the roast to cool in its own juices.

To mold the roast and clarify the jelly:
Degrease the roast jelly and the jelly made two days ago. Slowly melt the two jellies together, stirring continuously.
Beat the eggs, and add the broken shells. Pour the eggs into the hot jelly. When all the residue has risen to the surface, skim and pass through a very fine sieve. If the weather is hot, add more gelatin. Pour a little jelly into a meatloaf mold and let it set. Place one sage leaf in the bottom.

Setting the roast in aspic:
Remove the string and discard the strips of fat. Place the roast on the jelly in the bottom of the mold. Cover with the rest of the jelly and refrigerate. Unmold before serving.

French Fritters

Makes about 40 fritters
- 1 cup cold water
- 5½ tablespoons butter
- 1¼ cups flour
- 3 eggs
- A pinch of salt

To prepare Pâte à Choux (puff paste):
Place the butter in a saucepan with cold water and bring to a boil, then remove from heat. Pour in all the flour at once and beat vigorously with a wooden spatula to dissolve any possible lumps. When the mixture is smooth, cook 2 more minutes, then remove from heat. Beat in the eggs one at a time, add salt, then set aside to cool.

To fry the fritters:
Heat the oil (not too much—about 375°) in a deep-fat fryer.
Drop walnut-size balls of paste one at a time into the hot oil. The balls rise to the surface as they cook. Fry 10 minutes, turning occasionally. Place on a paper towel and sprinkle with confectioner's sugar.
The fritters are best served hot, but may be served lukewarm if need be.

Unmolded Caramel Custard

Serves 6
- 1 quart fresh whole milk
- 1 vanilla bean
- 6 eggs
- $\frac{3}{4}$ cup sugar
- 1 shot glass (1 tablespoon) rum, kirsch, or any other liquor that goes well with vanilla)
- 12 lumps sugar (large)
- 2 tablespoons cold water

To prepare the custard:
Boil the milk with the vanilla bean. Meanwhile, mix 3 whole eggs and 3 yolks with the sugar in a large bowl, stirring constantly to a smooth, thick, pale yellow cream. Flavor with the liquor and stir gently. Slowly pour the hot milk into the cream, beating vigorously with a wire whisk. Skim the surface and remove the vanilla bean. Allow to cool while the oven is preheating (300°) and you prepare the caramel.

To prepare the caramel:
Place the lumps of sugar and the cold water in a custard mold. Melt the sugar on low heat and caramelize until light brown. Remove from heat at once and spread the caramel around with a wooden spoon to coat the sides of the mold. Act quickly, because the caramel hardens as it cools.

To bake the custard:
As soon as the sides of the mold are cool enough to handle, pour in the egg mixture and bake about 35 minutes. The custard is done when a knife inserted in the middle comes out clean.
Allow to cool. When still slightly warm, place a serving dish over the mold, turn the two upside down in one quick motion, and carefully unmold the custard onto the dish. Serve with almond wafers or berries.

Madeleines

Makes 10 madeleines
- $\frac{1}{4}$ cup butter
- $\frac{1}{4}$ cup sugar
- 2 eggs
- $\frac{2}{3}$ cup flour
- $\frac{1}{2}$ teaspoon yeast (unless you use cake flour)
- Vanilla or orange flower water
- Lemon peel

Beat together well the butter and the sugar. Stir in the eggs one at a time, then add the flour, yeast, and vanilla or orange flower water. When the batter is smooth, pour into buttered and floured madeleine molds.
Bake in 350° oven 12 minutes.

Alternative recipe:
In a large bowl, mix together the egg yolks, sugar, flour, and softened butter. Add a finely ground lemon peel. Beat the egg whites until firm and fold into the mixture.
Bake as for recipe above.

Pears Bourdaloue

Serves 6
- 6 nice Williams or Packham pears
- A light syrup made with $\frac{1}{2}$ cup sugar, a dash of vanilla extract, and 1 cup water

For the frangipane:
- 3 cups milk
- 1 teaspoon vanilla extract
- 1 cup sugar
- 4 eggs
- 1 cup flour
- A pinch of salt
- $\frac{1}{4}$ cup butter
- A few drops of bitter almond extract
- 8 tablespoons crushed macaroons

To prepare the pears:
Halve pears, peel, and remove seeds.
Bring the syrup ingredients to a boil, and cook uncovered a few minutes.
Poach the pears in the syrup 10 minutes. Set aside.

To make the frangipane:
Boil the milk with the vanilla. Meanwhile, beat the sugar and the eggs together in a bowl with a wire whisk. Gradually add the flour and salt, blending well to obtain a smooth batter. Pour in the milk a little at a time, stirring vigorously to avoid lumps.
Transfer to a saucepan, set on low heat, and allow to thicken, stirring continuously.
Remove from heat. Stir in 6 tablespoons of the crushed macaroons together with the butter and bitter almond extract.

To serve:
Arrange the pears in an ovenproof serving dish. Pour the frangipane over them and sprinkle with the remaining crushed macaroons.
Brown 5 to 10 minutes in 400° oven until the macaroons are golden brown.

Camille Pissarro, *Still Life with Pears*, 1872
Private collection

Here Pissarro exploits different color effects: the yellow, green, and orange pears placed on the white tablecloth against a background of rose wallpaper. He seems interested above all in the decorative impact of the work.

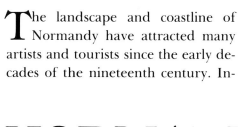

3

The landscape and coastline of Normandy have attracted many artists and tourists since the early decades of the nineteenth century. In-

NORMANDY

Detail from page 101

deed, Normandy could be seen as a training ground for Impressionism. Monet and Boudin were both brought up there; by 1862 they were painting landscapes in the open air around Le Havre with Jongkind. Here they pursued the art of land- and seascapes, taking into account the way in which the visual sensation of a place could be altered by shifting conditions of weather, atmosphere, and light. Monet freely acknowledged that his meeting with Boudin had opened his eyes so that for the first time he felt that he really understood nature.

In the wake of the Impressionists came increasing numbers of artists to the coastal stretch between Honfleur and Trouville, which became known

88

☐

Claude Monet, *Hôtel des Roches-Noires,*
***Trouville*, 1870**
Paris, Musée d'Orsay

The Hôtel des Roches-Noires was the finest deluxe
hotel in Trouville and attracted a fashionable and
wealthy clientele. The international attraction of the
hotel is suggested by Monet's inclusion of the French,
English, and American flags. The careful structuring
of the hotel façade, the walkway, flags, and figures is
disguised by the loose handling of paint and
summary treatment of forms.

as the "Barbizon of Normandy." In the middle of the nineteenth century, one of the most popular meeting places was the Saint-Siméon farm at Honfleur, where Mère Toutain and her daughter played host to successive waves of artists, including Boudin, Monet, Jongkind, Sisley, Pissarro, and Cézanne. In their letters these artists commented on the magnificent views from the terrace of the farmhouse, extolling the beauty of the surrounding countryside and vistas of the sea. For a small price they could enjoy the delights of Mère Toutain's cooking, which made the most of local produce and the specialties of the region. She was famed for her fish and shellfish dishes, as well as her Poularde à la Crème and homemade cider. The convivial atmosphere, engendered as much by the

Eugène Boudin, *The Saint-Siméon Farm*, 1860
Paris, private collection

In this view of the Saint-Siméon farm, presumably
done on site, it is tempting to speculate whether the
figures in this work are fellow artists discussing the
business of painting in the open air.

food and cider as by the intense conversations about the business of plein air painting, is captured in Boudin's *The Saint-Siméon Farm*.

At the farm, artists were undoubtedly aware (whether consciously or not) that in Normandy the landscape and the cuisine were inextricably linked. It is even true to say that the cuisine of this region has been shaped more than most by the food it produces. The cuisine has always relied heavily on the products of the sea as well as the three C's: cream, cider, and calvados. Any dish described as "à la Normande" would undoubtedly contain two of these ingredients. Similarly, the rich pasturelands support herds of black-and-white dairy cattle, the traditional symbol of Normandy's wealth and the source of some of its most famous products: cream, butter, and cheese.

Many Norman specialties use the heavy local cream. Typically, Sauce Normande (an accompaniment to many egg, fish, and chicken dishes) consisted of a roux made of butter and flour to which was added a bouillon enriched with cider, white wine, or egg yolks and finished with a dollop of cream and butter. Mère Toutain's Poularde à la Crème was a traditional dish of chicken with cream, as was Poulet Vallée d'Auge (see recipe) garnished with tiny onions. Pigs reared on windfalls from the

☐
Eugène Boudin, *Group of Painters at the Saint-Siméon Farm*, **c. 1860**
private collection

In 1867 Monet wrote to Frédéric Bazille from the Saint-Siméon farm, reporting that he was greatly enjoying the convivial company of his fellow artists. In this rapid watercolor sketch, Boudin has caught the relaxed jollity of their get-togethers with (from left) Jongkind, Émile Van Marcke, Monet, and Père Achard.

apple orchards would be ceremoniously killed by the local charcutier once a year and the resulting pork cooked à la Normande, generally with cream and apples.

There were delectable nuances in the preparation of duckling, a specialty of the Seine valley where the ducks were reared tethered to apple trees. In the traditional dish Canard à la Rouennaise (see recipe), the duck is smothered so that the blood is not lost and the meat retains more flavor. In the nineteenth century restaurateur Père Mechenet revived the use of the duck press for this dish.

Near Mont Saint-Michel, mutton and lamb were raised on the salt marsh pastures of the Cotentin peninsula, and in the last decades of the nineteenth century, the island was also noted for Mère Poularde's omelette. Manager of the hotel-restaurant Tête d'Or, Mère Poularde would never divulge the exact recipe for her phenomenally successful omelette, but it was said to contain the finest butter and eggs, its lightness explained by the proportion of whisked egg whites and a very short cooking time.

The abundance of butter in the cuisine leads one naturally to think of cheese and pastries. Because many Normand cheeses were made from double and triple cream, it is not surprising that they had a high fat content: Camembert, Pont L'évêque, Neufchâlet, Brillat-Savarin, and Coeur de Bray are some of these rich cheeses. The pastries were and are characterized by the richness of their butter content, including *sablés*, "sandy" or crumbly textured butter biscuits, and *bourdelots*, apple dumplings wrapped in butter pastry (when made with pears, they are called *douillons*).

Because it has been the premier apple-growing area in France, apples have figured largely in Norman cuisine. They were combined with pastries and used in desserts, of which the ambrosial Norman apple tarts have a flavor and richness unmatched by any other apple tart. The landscape is still dotted with apple and cider-apple trees, the fruit gathered late in the season and then pressed and blended before being left to ferment. The distilling of cider to make calvados is an old Norman tradition dating to the sixteenth century. Ideally, the cider should be aged for twelve to fifteen years in oak, although this is rarely done. The raw, highly alcoholic "young" calvados was more often used in the nineteenth century for the ritual of the Trou (literally "hole") Normand, a glass of calvados drunk as a digestive between courses.

Confectionery of the region included sugar apples and *duchesses* (a type of macaroon) from Rouen. The most delectable *mirlitons* (almond and cream tartlets filled with eggs, almonds, sugar, and cream) also came

Detail from page 94

Camille Pissarro, *The Apple Pickers*, 1886
Tokyo, Hara Museum

Pissarro made a number of studies of apple-picking and harvesting in Eragny. In this work he experimented with the decorative qualities of a square canvas. The simplified shapes of the three women recede in space. Our eye is further pulled back by the diagonal lines of the violet shadow (moving right from the center foreground) and the diagonal lines of the crops in the background, all of which give the painting a patterned flatness.

from Rouen. *Galets* (marzipan sweets) came from Le Havre and *croquettes* (small cakes) from Argentan. The meal could be completed with a glass of Bénédictine from Fécamp or yet another glass of calvados. Count Curnonsky, the "Prince of Gastronomes," wrote that an important meal in Normandy always commenced with a bouillon or pot-au-feu, then tripe, followed by mutton, after which there was a pause for the Trou Normand. With renewed appetites the diners would then fall upon roast veal and fowl, followed by desserts, coffee, and more calvados.

In 1864 Monet invited his friend Bazille to Honfleur so that they could paint the landscape and enjoy Mère Toutain's delicious cooking. Bazille was delighted with the local landscape as well as the seaside vistas, colorful local costume, and the hospitality of Monet's family and the people at the Saint-Siméon farm. He wrote home to his parents: "As soon as we arrived in Honfleur, we looked for landscape motifs. They were easy to find because the country is heaven. One could not see richer meadows and more beautiful trees; everywhere there are cows and horses at pasture. The sea, or rather the Seine broadening out, gives a delightful horizon to the masses of green ... We eat at the Saint-Siméon farm, situated on the cliff a little above Honfleur; it's there that we work and spend our days. The port of Honfleur and the costumes of the Normans with their cotton caps interest me greatly. I've been to Le Havre ... I had lunch with Monet's family; they are charming people."[11]

The distinctive headgear of the local women at the "port of Honfleur" can be seen in Boudin's sketch of *The Little Fish Market at Honfleur,* in which the artist has vividly captured the activity of the scene where the fish are being gutted, cleaned, and sold. Boudin's father was the captain of an Honfleur paddleboat, so the artist was at home in such surroundings. At this time Honfleur was a thriving seaport with a population of more than ten thousand, many of whom were engaged in shipbuilding and fishery work. The sketch is a reminder also of the importance of fish and shellfish in Norman cooking. Most of the fish was and still is caught

□

Eugène Boudin, *The Little Fish Market at Honfleur,* **c. 1859**
Honfleur, Musée Eugène Boudin

Boudin spent most of his working life painting the Norman landscape. His father was the captain of an Honfleur paddleboat, so this was a scene that the artist knew well.

in the English channel in an astounding variety: skate, sole, mackerel, turbot, mullet, gurnard, bream, and the incomparable Dover sole (cooked à la Normande with the addition of mussels, shrimps, oysters, and mushrooms and of course cream added to the velouté sauce at the end). Then there were the shellfish: oysters, clams, mussels, cockles and shrimps, scallops, and delicate rose-pink langoustines from along the Norman coast. Dieppe was noted for its small piquant mussels cooked either marinière, as in Moules Marinière (see recipe), or à la crème. Fish could be poached in a cider-laced *fumet* (literally "aroma," a heady and concentrated stock), and sauces were frequently embellished with mussels and shrimps.

Much of this seafood and other produce from Dieppe, Le Havre, and Rouen was transported to Paris via the Seine, the main arterial connection with the metropolis. Napoleon noted that Paris, Rouen, and Le

Claude Monet, *Étretat, la plage et la porte d'Amont*, 1883
Paris, Musée d'Orsay

Every year between 1883 and 1866, Monet painted in Étretat, famous for the chalk arches flanking its bays, the smallest of which, the Porte d'Amont, is shown here. Monet generally remained at Étretat after the summer crowds had left. Here he painted the turbulent waters with vigorous brush strokes—often from the safety of his hotel window.

Havre were but a single town with the Seine as its main street. For some of the artists who made their way to Normandy in the 1860s and 1870s, including Monet, Morisot, Renoir, and Sisley, Normandy was a continuation of their sketching expedition along the Seine. Since the middle of the nineteenth century, fishing villages up and down the channel coast were transformed into fashionable resorts for seaside vacations, attracting both a French and an English clientele.

The channel resorts also appealed to Manet, who, like other wealthy

97

□

Berthe Morisot, *Déjeuner sur l'herbe*
private collection

Morisot has once again turned to a domestic scene drawing from her own experience of family life with her husband Eugène Manet (the brother of the painter) and her daughter Julie, born in 1878. A keen proponent of painting in the open air, Morisot uses here spontaneous brush strokes, and seemingly random strokes of color.

Parisians during the 1860s enjoyed taking his family on a seaside vacation. He visited Trouville briefly in 1867, and in 1868 he took his family
to spend the summer at Boulogne, where he painted a number of modern life scenes of the harbor and pier at Boulogne and the tourist traffic
between France and England *(The Departure of the Folkestone Boat)*. Unlike

many artists who preferred to concentrate on outdoor scenes of seaside vacationers, Manet also painted family mealtimes. In *Luncheon in the Studio* he focused on the figure of his illegitimate son Léon Leenhoff, posed in front of the remains of an elaborate meal, while in the background a maid waits with a coffeepot. The food on the table is presented with deliberation and finesse. Is it a studio or a dining room?

As well as working in the open air alongside Jongkind and Boudin in the 1860s, from around 1870 Monet sought out the newly fashionable seaside resorts, such as Trouville, which were attracting large numbers of Parisian bourgeoisie who came to dine, to take the sea air and swim, and to promenade, as Boudin depicted them in his rather chilly paintings of the middle classes at leisure there. Contemporary guidebooks noted the attraction of fine sands, the exquisite countryside surrounding the town, its many elegant villas and mansions, and the good swimming facilities. Entrepreneurs had ensured further comfort and entertainment for the tourist in the form of hotels ranging from the comfortable to the grand, as well as a casino and café-concerts. Many commented on the Parisian atmosphere of the place. There were also polo matches, children's theatre, and regattas.

Often it was the painters and writers who put these places on the map and visually prepared visitors for their experience. In the 1870s Monet (in financial straits, as usual) was also interested in painting subjects already proven to be modish and popular that would appeal to prospective clients.

Together with his wife Camille (they had been married on June 8), Monet arrived in Trouville in July 1870 intending to spend the summer there. They stayed at the Hotel Tivoli, one of the less fashionable hotels away from the seafront, and were joined by Boudin and his wife in mid-August. Here the two couples enjoyed all the delights that the town could offer, including the local cuisine and seafood specialties. The two men could also combine their recreational activities with painting. Boudin painted the vacationers gathered along the sandy beach, while Monet continued his interest in modern life subjects and painted the fashionable tourists at leisure.

In *Hôtel des Roches-Noires, Trouville,* Monet depicted the premier hotel in town, known as "the king of the Norman coast," which had been named after the area's seaweed-and-mussel-covered rocks. Capturing some of the metropolitan elegance for which the hotel was noted, Monet depicted the guests taking the air, relaxing, and idly conversing. The low vantage point increases the amount of blue sky (and sea) so that the overriding

impression is of a serene and carefree existence. The hotel boasted all the amenities one could expect to find in a first-class Parisian hotel and was compared with the Grand Hôtel on the boulevard des Capucines (which Monet was to paint in 1873). In addition to the one hundred and fifty guest rooms, there was a concert hall, a café, and a smart restaurant where as well as making the most of local produce, the Parisian chef would serve more elaborate dishes designed to appeal to Parisian taste

Édouard Manet, *Luncheon in the Studio*, 1868
Munich, Bayerische Staatsgemäldesammlungen–Neue Pinakothek

Manet, who spent a number of summers vacationing on the channel coast, painted this work while he was staying at Boulogne-sur-Mer with his wife and son Léon Leenhoff (in the foreground). Manet's acute

attention to detail is evident in the deliberation and virtuosity with which he has treated the still life that signals the concluded meal and the weaponry on the chair.

and to the international clientele. For many guests their stay at the Roches-Noires was not only a seaside vacation with all its attendant attractions, but also a gourmet getaway. Here they could sample the artistry of the chef and his team of sous-chefs and revel in eating the kind of food beyond the skills of the cook at home.

In the decade after his summer in Trouville, Monet did not paint seaside tourism, concentrating more on the landscape motifs along the Seine at

Claude Monet, *Lunch under the Tent, Giverny*, 1888
private collection

In 1883 Monet settled in Giverny (just inside the Norman border) with Alice Hoschedé, his future wife. He had an awning put up so that he could enjoy summer meals outside with his family. In this loosely painted work, he depicts Alice Hoschedé at the lunch table.

Argenteuil, Vétheuil, and then turning to his great series: *Gare Saint-Lazare, Rouen*, and *The Poplars*. Camille Monet died in 1879, and in 1883 Monet settled with Alice Hoschedé (who later became his wife) in Giverny, which was just inside the Norman border. Here he devoted himself to his art, his family, gardening, and the pleasures of the table. He also began at this time to enjoy greater financial security.

At Giverny the Café Baudy (established in 1886) attracted numerous artist-visitors and the owners, Lucien and Angélina, apparently had a soft spot for artists. The café was well run and the food was excellent. The cooking was basically cuisine grand-mère, with the addition of English and American dishes—like Christmas pudding, stuffed spareribs, and Thanksgiving recipes—to please the American and English guests. The Baudys even had a studio built, and Madame Baudy became the agent for Lefèvre and Foinet and sold paint, canvas, and brushes on the premises. Foremost among the artists was a colony of American painters who began settling at Giverny in the mid-1880s, initially unaware that Monet lived there. At first Monet did not mind the presence of so many outsiders and would stop by the café for a drink and a chat, but eventually it seems he found their presence noisy and disruptive and stayed away, preferring to see his friends at home (some of whom, like Cézanne and Cassatt, stayed at the Baudy inn). In the late 1880s he formed a close friendship with the American artist John Singer Sargent, and they painted together at Giverny in 1888.

The Monets were keen gourmets and their cuisine was diverse. French home cooking, local Norman dishes like Sole à la Normande, and classic French dishes appeared regularly at their table, and they apparently enjoyed the English ritual of afternoon tea. Their personal cookbooks also included recipes from artist and writer friends, as well as reflecting Monet's travels around France and further afield to England and along the Mediterranean coast.

During the summer, an awning was put up in the garden with a long table so that the family could eat and entertain outdoors. Both Monet and Sargent painted similar views of Alice seated at the lunch table. In *Lunch under the Tent, Giverny*, Monet evokes his sensuous enjoyment of taking meals outdoors in the garden, reminding us of both the pleasures of dining alfresco and the continual interweaving of his own passions: painting, gardening, and fine dining.

Dieppe Fish Stew

Serves 4

Fish:
- 1 quart mussels
- 4 scallops in their shells
- $\frac{1}{2}$ lb. angler or monkfish
- $\frac{1}{2}$ lb. fillet of sole
- $\frac{1}{2}$ lb. fillet of turbot
- $\frac{1}{2}$ lb. fillet of brill
- 8 langoustines, or large prawns

Fish stock:
- 1 carrot
- 1 leek
- 2 shallots
- 2 cloves garlic
- $\frac{1}{2}$ tablespoon butter
- 2 tablespoons oil
- Trimmings of the above fish (heads and bones)
- 1 bay leaf, fresh thyme leaves
- 1 lb. small crabs
- Salt and pepper
- 2 cups dry white wine

Sauce:
- $\frac{1}{4}$ cup butter
- 1 cup crème fraîche or whipping cream
- 1 teaspoon potato flour
- A dash of curry powder
- A dash of cayenne pepper

To make the stock:
Mince the vegetables. Melt the butter with the oil in a cast-iron pot, add the vegetables, and sauté about 10 minutes. Add the fishheads and bones with the thyme and bay leaves. Crush the crabs in a mortar and add to the pot. Add salt and pepper.
When the crabs have turned red, pour in the white wine and 1 cup water, and cook 30 minutes. Pass through a sieve.

To prepare the fish and shellfish:
Steam open the mussels in a saucepan, filter the juices, and add the juices to the stock.
Open the scallop shells and rinse them under cold water.
Quarter the fish. Tuck the langoustines' claws into their tails so they straighten out.

To cook the fish:
Bring the stock to a boil.
Place the fish in a metal basket, lower the heat under the stock, and then plunge the fish into the stock. This will stop the boiling. Slowly bring back to a boil and switch off the heat at once. Allow to rest 5 minutes. Remove the fish and keep warm with the mussels.

To make the sauce:

Heat 2 cups of the stock without bringing to a boil. Beat in with a wire whisk the butter and cream, then the potato flour diluted in a small amount of warm stock. Add the curry powder, cayenne pepper, and salt if needed.

To serve:

Warm the plates and fill each with 1 piece of every fish, 2 langoustines, 1 scallop, and a few mussels. Spoon the sauce over the fish and serve at once.

Rouen Duck

The difficulty in this recipe is that you must use a duck press to crush the carcass. Although you could crush it between two cutting boards, it is exerting and, in this case, the recipe cannot be completed in front of the guests the way it is done in restaurants. Otherwise, it is quite simple.

Serves 4
- Two 2-lb. ducklings, wild if possible
- 12 minced shallots
- ½ cup butter
- 4 tablespoons oil
- Salt and pepper
- ½ cup red wine
- 2 slices toasting bread

To prepare the ducklings:
Flambé the ducklings carefully to eliminate all feathers.
Peel and mince the shallots.

To cook the ducklings:
Roast the ducklings in a very hot oven (450°) about 10 minutes so they are still rare. Meanwhile, sauté the shallots in butter and oil.
Remove the ducklings from the oven, carve out the drumsticks, and finish cooking on the grill.
Carve out the breasts, cut them into thin strips, and collect the blood into a bowl.
Arrange the shallots in a warm ovenproof serving dish and arrange the breast strips over them. Season with salt and pepper.
Press the carcasses, squeezing out as much blood as possible. Pour the blood into the bowl and add the red wine. Pour over the breast strips and bake in 450° oven while you brown the two slices of bread in butter and oil. Cut the croutons diagonally.
Remove the breasts from the oven. Place the four croutons on the sides of the dish and the four drumsticks at each end. Serve.

Mussels Marinière

- 1 quart mussels
- 1 shallot
- Parsley
- Thyme and bay leaves
- 1 cup white wine
- Pepper
- 2 tablespoons butter

Wash and scrub the mussels meticulously.
Chop the shallots and parsley.
Place the mussels in a kettle and cook with the shallots, chopped parsley, thyme, bay leaves, and white wine. Add pepper. The

mussels are done when they are open and flavored by the other ingredients. Remove from heat immediately, set aside, and keep warm. Pour the cooking juices into a saucepan, add chopped parsley and butter, blend and stir over high heat until the liquid is reduced by one-half.

Spoon over the mussels and serve at once.

Auge Valley Chicken Stew

Serves 4
- 1 large chicken
- 2 carrots
- 1 shallot
- 4 pippin apples
- 1 lb. white mushrooms
- $\frac{1}{2}$ cup butter
- $\frac{1}{4}$ cup oil
- 2 onions: one sliced, the other studded with cloves
- 1 cup dry white wine
- 1 clove garlic
- Thyme and bay leaves
- Salt and freshly ground pepper
- 1 cup crème fraîche or whipping cream
- 1 shot glass (1 tablespoon) calvados
- 3 egg yolks

To prepare the vegetables:
Peel and dice the carrots, slice the shallot, and peel and quarter the apples. Wash the mushrooms and mince.

To prepare the chicken for cooking:
Flambé the chicken carefully and quarter.

To cook:
In a cast-iron casserole, lightly brown the chicken in half the butter and 2 tablespoons oil. When all pieces are nicely golden, add the carrots, shallots, and the sliced onion and cook a few minutes. Pour the white wine and 1 cup water over the chicken, then add the clove-studded onion, garlic, thyme, bay leaves, and salt and pepper. Cover and simmer over low heat 40 minutes.

Remove from heat, arrange the pieces of chicken in an ovenproof serving dish, and keep warm. Pass the cooking liquid through a sieve. Set the vegetables aside and keep warm. Meanwhile, melt the remaining butter in a skillet with the oil, add the apples, and cook until just lightly brown on all sides. Remove the apples from the skillet and arrange them around the chicken. Keep the dish warm in the oven.

Sauté the mushrooms until they have lost all their juices. Set aside to add to the sauce.

To make the sauce:
Pour the strained cooking liquid into a saucepan and set over medium heat. With a whisk, beat in the cream, the calvados, and the egg yolks in that order. Simmer in a double boiler until it has thickened to a light cream. Stir in the mushrooms and vegetables, discarding the clove-studded onion. Adjust seasoning.

Remove the dish from the oven, spoon some of the sauce over the chicken, and pour the remaining sauce into a sauceboat and serve.

Puff Pastry Cake with Jam

Serves 4
- $\frac{1}{2}$ lb. puff pastry dough
- 3 tablespoons strawberry, raspberry, or blackberry jam
- 1 egg
- $\frac{1}{2}$ cup crème fraîche or whipping cream

To prepare the puff pastry dough:
Make three "turns" with the dough: roll out the dough into a rectangle with a rolling pin. Fold into three. Rotate this "wallet" one quarter turn.
Roll out the dough again *in the same direction as the first time*. Again fold into three and rotate one quarter turn.

Repeat this procedure once more for a total of three quarter turns.

To make the cake:
Divide the dough in half.
Roll out half in all directions into a circle about $\frac{1}{3}$-inch thick. Place on a buttered and floured cookie sheet, and spread with jam.
Cover with the other half of the dough. Seal the edges and carve in decorative lines on the edges and top. Brush with a beaten egg. Bake in 400° oven about 25 minutes.
Serve warm (but not hot) with a bowl of crème fraîche.

Detail from page 116

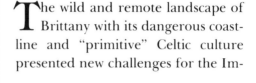

4

The wild and remote landscape of Brittany with its dangerous coast-line and "primitive" Celtic culture presented new challenges for the Im-

BRITTANY

pressionists in the 1880s. Brittany's attraction for artists was primarily in terms of the old rather than the new, so that it did not have the appeal of modernity that had drawn the Impressionists to Paris, the Seine, and the Norman coastline. In the last quarter of the nineteenth century Brittany was still largely untouched by industrialization in spite of the advent of the railway and the building of new roads. To the visitor, the western half of the peninsula—Lower Brittany, which was also known as Bretagne bretonnante (Breton Brittany)—was even more remote and had retained many of its ancient traditions.

In *Breton Folk* (1878) the English writer Henry Blackburn characterized

□
Berthe Morisot,
The Harbor at Lorient, 1869
Washington, National Gallery of Art

At this time Lorient, on the Atlantic coast, attracted increasing numbers of Parisian tourists. Like Monet, Morisot was interested in painting the landscape of tourism, and her modishly dressed sister Edma adds a sophisticated accent to this depiction of a fishing village.

the charms of Brittany as being contingent upon the simplicity of life, the hard landscape which seemed to resist the efforts of men to "tame" it, its strong folklore tradition, unusual customs, and the picturesque inhabitants in their national costume. He felt that Brittany offered more for artists than Normandy: "Rougher and wilder than Normandy, more thinly populated and less visited by tourists, Brittany offers better opportunity for outdoor study and more suggestive scenes for the painter." Brittany's cultural differences fascinated artists. The people were not French but Celts and had a language and a culture that was separate from the rest of France (the Breton language continued to be spoken in the nineteenth century). To the visitor Brittany seemed to be locked in the past, and this too was part of its nostalgic appeal.

The landscape was one of contrasts: the jagged and hazardous coastline relieved by some of the finest natural harbors, such as Brest and Lorient. Similarly the rocky lands to the west and center of Brittany are unlike the milder, more fertile Pays Nantais to the south. These geographic factors affected the region's produce. Apart from the gastronomic excellence of the seafood from right around the coast, there was the fine salt meadow mutton produced in the northwest—a region also noted for its pungent game. In central Brittany the produce has traditionally been that of subsistence agriculture: chestnuts, dried beans, and buckwheat. As none of these can be used for making bread, the Bretons substituted crêpes or galettes for bread.

In the north not far from the coast, some of the best farming was developed in the nineteenth century. Here market gardening still flourishes to produce artichokes, cauliflowers, potatoes, peas, beans, and fine strawberries. The area around the Pays Nantais is noted for its butter and white wine, which are combined with vinegar and shallots in a white butter sauce to serve with pike from the Loire in a dish known as Brochet à Beurre Blanc (see recipe).

The description *à la Bretonne* implies a flavorful and filling cuisine, signifying that the dish is made up of haricots, a legume of the region, or is accompanied by beans, as in the leg of mutton dish Gigot de Mouton à la Bretonne.

For the Impressionists, Brittany meant different things. Both Eugène Boudin and Berthe Morisot had family to visit there. Boudin, whose wife came from Brittany, painted landscapes all over the northern coast and in the western Finistère region. Morisot's sister, Edma, lived in various Brittany towns after her marriage to a naval officer. On her trips to see her sister, Berthe painted the family at home. Beyond the confines of

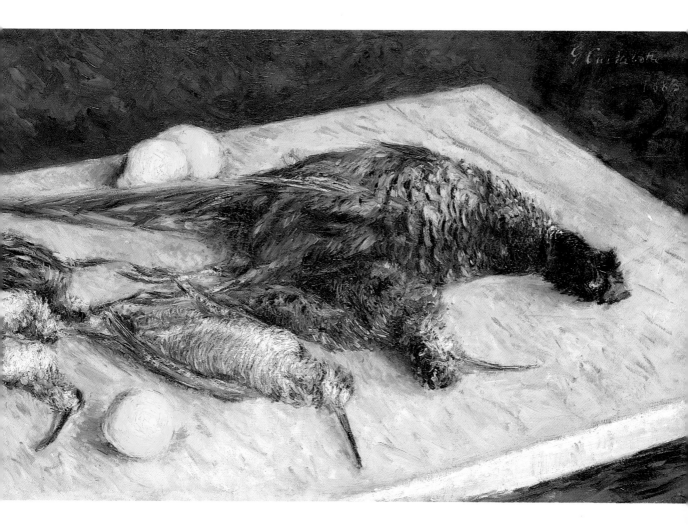

Edma's house and garden, Morisot (unlike most other painters) treated the Brittany landscape as a modern site. In *The Harbor at Lorient* Edma posed as the woman in the foreground, thereby adding a fashionable and contemporary accent to the painting. Renoir took his family for seaside vacations to Brittany, often stopping at Pont-Aven (which by then was established as an artist's colony), where he stayed at the Hôtel des Voyageurs. A specialty of the hotel was the Omelette au Rhum, which was brought into the dining room on a flaming platter—apparently to great applause from the assembled company. He also painted the scenery around Pont-Aven, searching out a gentler, more cultivated landscape for Impressionist treatment.

In the autumn of 1886 Monet spent some months at Belle-Ile, a remote and windswept island off the southern coast of the Brittany peninsula. In

115

□
Gustave Caillebotte. *Pheasants and Woodcocks on a Marble Table,* 1883
Springfield, Museum of Fine Arts

Here the intense yellow of the lemons serves to "lift" not only the browns and orange/gold of the birds laid out on the marble slab, but also the tone of the painting on a more abstract level—as symbols of life rather than death.

spite of the lack of home comforts (he particularly missed the Giverny cuisine), he became obsessed by the landscape and wrote to Berthe Morisot describing Belle-Ile as a "terrible, sinister, yet beautiful country." The beauty of the ocean compelled him to work at all hours in all weathers. The result was a series of trenchant views of rock and sea: a forceful reminder of the perils of this Atlantic coastline and the appalling casualties at sea.

Monet lodged with a fisherman, J. M. Marec, who also cooked his meals for four francs a day. At Père Marec's auberge he met the journalist

116

Eugène Boudín, *Still Life with Lobster on a White Tablecloth*, c. 1853–1856
Atlanta, High Museum of Art

Boudin's deliberate placement of the objects in this traditional mealtime composition and his choice of lobster, glassware, china, and ceramic pot with scenic detail, suggest that he had been looking closely at seventeenth-century Flemish still lifes, as well as at Chardin. The painting was designed to appeal to the more refined tastes of the regional bourgeoisie, who were Boudin's patrons in the 1850s.

Gustave Geffroy, who in 1924 published *Claude Monet, sa vie, son temps, son oeuvre*. In his letters, Monet complained to Alice Hoschedé of the endless diet of fish and lobster (the butcher and baker only called once a week) and wrote of his longing for the culinary delights of the Café Riche. This situation improved once he met John Peter Russell, an Australian painter living in Brittany. Apart from enjoying the company of a fellow artist, Monet was thrilled by the excellent meals prepared by Russell's cook.

Certainly Monet's weariness with Breton lobster was not shared by others, and Brittany's seafood continues to be noted for its high quality, flavor, and ease of preparation. The plentiful and various shellfish include scallops, clams, crabs, oysters, and lobsters, which traditionally have been cooked simply. For lobsters, the standard treatment was to boil the smaller ones and bake the large ones. Scallops were frequently cooked with cider—a Norman specialty. In the seventeenth and eighteenth centuries Nantes was the center for the French spice trade to the Orient, and Coquilles Saint-Jacques Nantais was a traditional dish of sautéed spiced scallops.

Brittany has an abundant supply of fish: sole, turbot, and sea bass. Humbler fish like mackerel, whiting, and eel could be simmered together to make the memorable Breton version of bouillabaisse known as cotriade, which derives its name from the *côte* (coast) where it originated. Breton sailors were the first to make cotriade, using any unwanted part of the catch and cooking the stew at sea. On land it is usually made with a mixture of fish cooked with onions and potatoes and seasoned with bay leaves and thyme. In the nineteenth century it was served in much the same way as bouillabaisse and pot-au-feu. The liquid was poured over slices of bread and taken as a soup, and the fish and vegetables were eaten separately as the next course.

The picturesque coastal fishing town of Concarneau, which attracted numerous artists in the 1880s, was best known for its sardine industry (which was such an integral feature of town life that one artist dubbed the place Sardineopolis). Sardines were eaten fried with boiled potatoes. Traditionally the most hazardous fishing has been on the oceangoing ships that trawled the Atlantic for salt cod and tuna. The Ile d'Ouessant (or Ushant in English), a desolate outcrop of rock rising out of the sea, is France's most westerly point and the departure point for much of this kind of fishing. Because of the high death toll among Ouessant sailors, a special symbolic service was established for those drowned at sea and the women habitually wore mourning. Some artists were drawn to Brittany with the object of depicting the harshness of peasant subsistence and their customs. Charles Cottet's *In the Country by the Sea* represented the grimmer side of life: the central panel of the triptych shows the funeral meal. On such occasions the food was hearty: seafood and meat unadorned with sauces, as well as crêpes and fars (batter puddings).

Probably the most renowned Breton culinary specialty are crêpes, which are known as *galettes* in eastern Brittany and have been used in a variety of ways. Savory crêpes were made with buckwheat flour and often took the place of bread. They could be wrapped around an egg, a slice of ham, sausage, cheese, sardines—or in any number of ways to create a filling and tasty meal. Wheat flour was used to make sweet pancakes. Traditionally these crêpes made up the whole meal. The first were chopped into the broth as *soupe*, the second spread with butter, and the third, with butter and sugar or jam. The more refined lacy-thin Crêpes Dentelles of Quimper are related to Crêpes Suzette (see recipe).

Fars and porridges were also substantial Breton fare. Far Breton (see recipe), flavored with prunes or raisins, was the most popular. Other

118

Charles Cottet, *In the Country by the Sea*, 1898
Paris, Musée d'Orsay

Cottet visited Brittany regularly and concerned himself with the portrayal of its harshness and melancholy. This painting is one of a series done to record different aspects of life on the Breton island of Ouessant.

desserts included *kouign-aman* (a rich yeast cake) and *maingaux,* a whipped cream dessert from Rennes.

Gauguin noted wryly that this kind of Breton fare was "food that made you fatter on the spot." In 1886, having decided that he needed to escape Paris, he settled in Pont-Aven at Madame Gloanec's auberge, which was known for extending credit to artists. Pont-Aven and nearby Concarneau had already attracted an international clientele: Americans, English, and Scandinavians. These were mainly realist artists who wished to paint the rigors of peasant life. At this stage, Gauguin (who had been working with Pissarro and Cézanne at Pontoise) was still employing Impressionist techniques.

Like many other artists, Gauguin ignored the fact that Brittany was becoming a tourist attraction. (It was also becoming more prosperous agriculturally, owing to improved methods of farming.) Instead he aimed

119

Édouard Manet, *Fish and Shrimps,* 1864
Pasadena, Norton Simon Museum

This is part of a series of still lifes in which Manet focused on a single object, apparently to express its material presence. This owes as much to the simplified composition as it does to the dramatic highlighting of the fish against the dark background and sideboard.

to present what he saw as the essence of Brittany and like many approached the place and its people in terms of mythologized notions of the primitive. In *Haymaking* he abandoned naturalism in favor of a simplification of color and shape with a deliberate flattening of space to create a powerful image of Breton life: the women in traditional costume (many of whom were paid by the artist to dress like this) are shown working the land, their rhythmic movements suggesting repetition and continuity. This painting was a deliberate move away from naturalistic representation, the spatial contraction and juxtaposition of colored shapes reminding us of the impact of Japanese prints on the Impressionists.

L'Auberge Gloanec, Pont Aven
Photo: Roger-viollet

The Gloanec Inn run by Marie-Jeanne Gloanec was host to numerous artists who made their way to Pont-Aven in the late nineteenth century, including Gauguin and Paul Sérusier. Here Gauguin is seated in the first row, second from the left.

Paul Gauguin, *Haymaking*, 1889
London, Courtauld Institute Galleries

This is one of two haymaking scenes made by Gauguin in July 1889. Because he has avoided naturalistic spatial recession, we read the painting vertically and in terms of simplified color zones, in which he employs a sequence of parallel strokes.

Paul Gauguin, *Haymaking*, 1889
London, Courtauld Institute Galleries

Gauguin's approach here particularly suited his desire to portray the spiritual qualities of life in Brittany.

At Pont-Aven, Gauguin was joined by a younger group of artists including Émile Bernard and Paul Sérusier. Their increasing rejection of naturalism and Gauguin's domineering personality antagonized many other artists, particularly those staying at the Pension Gloanec. This tension was resolved only by the instigation of two sittings at dinner: one for the *pompiers* (academic hacks) and one for the Impressionists (as they were still known). As usual the artists covered the walls with their paintings, but one elderly French painter threatened to leave if a painting by Gauguin was hung in the dining room. This may be why Gauguin signed his *Still Life: Fête Gloanec* "Madeleine Bernard," using the name of Bernard's little sister. (The still life was painted for Madame Gloanec's birthday.) Gauguin has again avoided naturalism in preference for a more abstracted ar

121

rangement of shape and color. The shades of orange, yellow, and green of the bouquet of flowers, the fruit, and the cake are bounded along the lower edge by a black line that marks the edge of the table—again recalling Japanese prints. The painting has a highly decorative appearance and operates also on a more abstract level. The orange and gold tones combined with the black give it the appearance of a precious lacquered object.

By the late 1880s Pont-Aven had become unbearably overcrowded, not only with hordes of artists and students, but also with tourists who had read the books and seen the paintings and now wished to see for themselves the meeting of bohemian and folk cultures.

Julia Guillou, the proprietor of the Hôtel des Voyageurs, advertised her hotel in England, offering sketching excursions and French conversation for young lady artists. Many seemed to come more for the social life than with the serious intention of painting, and there were complaints about the lack of metropolitan delicacies (such as champagne, ice cream, and lemonade) and the exorbitant price of lemons in Pont-Aven.

In October 1889 Gauguin moved away from the noise and disturbances to Le Pouldu a few miles away, where he stayed until the end of that year, returning the following summer. The Scottish artist Archibald Standish Hartrick later summed up the character of the place: "For dramatic strangeness, that was a wonder of a place; . . . Imagine a country of gigantic sand dunes, like the mountainous waves of a solid sea, between

122

Paul Gauguin, *Still Life: Fête Gloanec*, 1889
Orléans, Musée des Beaux-Arts

Page 123: detail

This innovative still life was a birthday present for Marie-Jeanne Gloanec the owner of the Gloanec Inn. Gauguin has abandoned a naturalistic treatment of space for this frontal view of a tabletop seen from above, on which he has placed the birthday "gifts": the bouquet of flowers in their white frill, the cake, and fruit. The work suggests the influence of Japanese wood-block prints, in the strong black contour in the foreground and the arbitrary juxtaposition of objects.

which appeared glimpses of the Bay of Biscay and the Atlantic rollers. All this peopled by a savage looking race . . . and with women in black dresses, who wore the great black coif."

Gauguin stayed at the Auberge des Grands-Sables, where he was given a free hand to decorate the walls of the inn with brightly colored works. One visiting artist thought that the commonplace had been transformed into the Temple of Apollo. Gauguin and his friends soon fell into a regular working pattern: breakfast at seven, followed by hard work until lunch at eleven thirty, then dinner at seven, followed by conversation, music, or a game before heading for bed at nine o'clock.

**Camille Pissarro, *The Pork Butcher*, 1883
London, Tate Gallery**

Pissarro's studies of rural life either celebrate harvesting or apple-picking in a rural arcadia or comprise more realistic studies, such as this one in which he portrays everyday life in the marketplace.

Gauguin returned to Pont-Aven in the spring of 1894 to find that the place had changed and his reception at the Auberge des Grands-Sables was far from friendly. His hopes for a simple life in beautiful surroundings and for good sustaining meals were disappointed. This was to be his last trip to Brittany, and the following year he went back to Tahiti once again in search of a mythic and primitive paradise.

125

□

**Paul Gauguin, *Still Life with Ham*, 1889
Washington, The Phillips Collection**

Gauguin probably painted this work at Pouldu. The work has a strongly decorative presence that owes as much to his careful structuring as to the complementary colors. The concentric circles of the ham, plate, and tabletop are held by the dark vertical stripes in the background, and then pulled together by the tapering legs of the table.

Pike with Butter Sauce

Serves 6
- 1 large 3-lb. pike
- 1 quart salted water
- 1 onion, minced
- 1 carrot, sliced
- 1 leek, sliced
- 1 celery stalk, chopped
- 1 bunch parsley
- Thyme, fennel, and bay leaves
- 2 cups white wine
- Peppercorns

Sauce:
- 5 shallots
- 1 cup wine vinegar
- $\frac{1}{2}$ lb. (2 sticks) butter, chilled
- Salt and pepper

The pike is cooked in broth (court bouillon), trimmed, and served with a butter sauce.

To cook the fish:
In a fish kettle, add the onion, carrot, leek, and celery stalk to 1 quart salted water. Add parsley, thyme, fennel, and bay leaves, and simmer 15 minutes. Stir in 2 cups white wine and cook 15 minutes more.

Plunge the pike into the liquid. Add the peppercorns (which shouldn't cook too long). If the fish is very big, you must allow the broth to cool before you immerse the fish in it, so that the pike absorbs all the aroma of the liquid.

As soon as the broth comes to a boil, switch off the heat and allow to cool. This way the fish cooks gently without risk of coming apart.

To make the sauce:
Mince the shallots and drop them into a saucepan containing the wine vinegar and 1 cup of the strained broth, and boil slowly 5 minutes until liquid is reduced by half. Remove from heat.

Dice the chilled butter and add it to the sauce, whipping vigorously by hand to a smooth paste. Season with salt and pepper and transfer to a warm sauceboat. Keep warm until ready to serve.

Rib of Beef with Buckwheat Mashed Potatoes

Serves 4
- One 3-lb. rib of beef
- Coarse salt and freshly ground pepper
- Thyme leaves
- 1 tablespoon oil
- 1 lb. good quality potatoes
- 1 cup buckwheat flour
- 2 cups cold water
- 1 egg
- $\frac{1}{2}$ cup salted butter, melted
- Salt and pepper

To cook the rib of beef:
Season each side of the rib with the coarse salt, pepper, and thyme.
Place in an ovenproof dish and coat with the oil.
Bake in 350° oven, allowing 15 minutes for the first pound and 10 minutes for each additional pound (35 minutes for a 3-lb. rib). Turn the meat when it is halfway done. When done, allow the beef rib to stand in warm oven 10 minutes so that the meat tightens back.

To make the potatoes:
While the rib is roasting, cook the potatoes in boiling water 20 minutes. Dissolve the buckwheat flour in 2 cups cold water, bring to a boil, and allow to thicken a few minutes, stirring continuously.
When the potatoes are done, peel them and mash with a potato-masher, then stir in the buckwheat mixture.
With a wooden spoon, mix in the egg, then the melted butter. Add salt and pepper to taste (the salted butter may provide enough salt).

To serve:
Lift the beef rib out of the dish.
Deglaze the dish with boiling water, and pour the juices in a sauceboat.
Carve the rib into slices.
Add the juices from the carving board to the sauceboat.
Serve the rib slices with the buckwheat potatoes and the sauce.

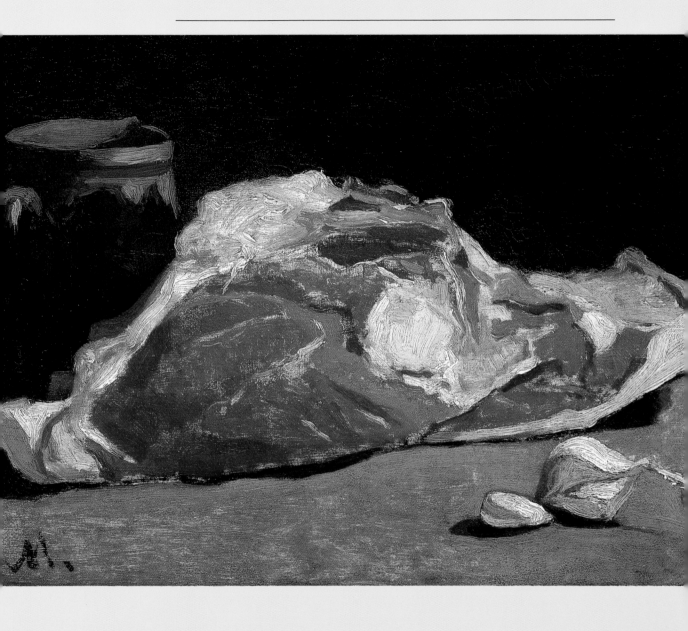

□
Claude Monet, *Still Life: Side of Beef,* **c. 1864**
Paris, Musée d'Orsay

Monet rarely painted still lifes in the 1860s. This
work may have been done after he had seen
Manet's interpretations of the subject, as there are
similarities in approach, such as the simplicity of
composition, liquid handling of paint, and the way
he suggests the physical presence of the beef.

Breton Prune Cake

Serves 4
- ½ lb. pitted prunes
- 2 cups tea
- 2 shot glasses (2 tablespoons) rum
- 1 cup flour
- 4 eggs
- 5 tablespoons sugar
- 2 cups milk

To make the filling:
Soak the prunes 2 hours in the tea and half the rum. (For best results, use moist prunes rather than dry ones.)

To make the batter:
Put the flour in a bowl and break any lumps with a fork.
With a wire whisk, beat in the eggs one at a time, then add the remaining rum and the milk, beating vigorously to eliminate all lumps.

To bake:
Preheat oven to 350°.
Butter and flour a round mold or ovenproof dish on all sides.
Arrange the prunes in the dish and pour the batter over them.
Cover and bake about 40 minutes.
Unmold and serve lukewarm.

Strawberry Sherbet

As a dessert or a side dish, sherbet used to be made in an ice-cream churn surrounded with crushed ice, where it would thicken under the combined effects of cold and pressure. The modern ice-cream maker is a more practical appliance, but you can also make a good sherbet in your refrigerator freezer.

Serves 6
- 2 lbs. shiny ripe strawberries
- Juice of ½ lemon
- 2 cups water
- 2½ cups sugar
- 1 oz. whipped cream
- A few whole fresh strawberries and/or other red berries and a twig of fresh mint to garnish

To make the sherbet:
Wash, hull, and dry the strawberries. Purée finely through a food mill and immediately mix together the pulp and the lemon juice.

Édouard Manet, *Basket of Strawberries*, 1882
New York, Metropolitan Museum of Art

Manet's still lifes of the 1880s often employ more overtly Impressionist treatment (possibly as a result of seeing Monet's interpretation of the subject). Here he uses high-keyed color and loose brushwork to evoke the transient pleasures of the fruit.
Detail from page 135

Bring the water to a boil in a heavy-bottom pot, pour in the sugar all at once, lower the heat, and simmer until you have a smooth syrup.

Remove from heat and quickly add the strawberry pulp to the syrup, stirring with a wooden spoon.

Pour this mixture into an ice-cream maker or a freezerproof dish, removing the dish from the freezer every hour and stirring with a fork 5 minutes to avoid crystallization and ensure a smooth consistency. With either method, bring out the sherbet half an hour before serving and carefully fold in the whipped cream, then chill again.

To serve:
If you are not using an ice-cream maker, dip the dish in warm water before unmolding the sherbet. Place sherbet in a serving dish and garnish with whole berries and fresh mint leaves.

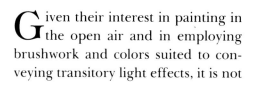

Detail from page 135

5

PROVENCE

Given their interest in painting in the open air and in employing brushwork and colors suited to conveying transitory light effects, it is not surprising that many Impressionists were drawn to Provence in the 1880s and 1890s. With the exception of Cézanne, they tended to concentrate either on the coastal strip or the inland region. In 1888 van Gogh came south and settled in Arles with the dream of establishing an artists' colony there. At this time Cézanne was developing his mature style in the environs of his native Aix-en-Provence. The landscapes of Monet, Renoir, and Signac capture the vibrating colors, sunlight, and sensuality of the coast.

Travelers in ancient times had commented on the beauty and variety of the landscape. In 1701 an English visitor wrote of "Provence, where all

☐

Vincent van Gogh,
Café Terrace at Night, 1888 (detail)
Otterlo, Rijksmuseum Kröller-Müller

Once again van Gogh has used complementary colors (orange and blue) side by side to highlight the brightly illuminated café in the Place du Forum, Arles, against the surrounding deep blue of the night sky.

our senses were ever cloyed with an immense variety of the most agreeable and charming objects. I fancied it to be one great Garden, where the Rival Products of Nature seemed to contend for the Masterdom. The fields and cultivated hills are stor'd with Vines, Almonds, Olives, Figs, Oranges and Pomegranates: and the Waste Ground (if I may so call it) is overspread with Rosemary, Time, Marjoram, Lavender, Myrtil, and divers other odiferous and medicinal Plants. In a word, it's the most fruitful and delectable Province on this side of the Alps, and justly stiled the paradise of France."

Provence remains a richly diverse region in terms of its landscape, produce, and cuisine, but because the coastal belt is cut off from the interior by the mountain ranges along the coast, it can broadly be separated into these two regions. (Such a distinction is crude and it is worth pointing out that there are subtle alterations in cuisine from town to town.) The intertwining of the landscape, its produce, and cuisine is best summed up by the description of Provence as the "land of the olive." The olive continues to shape the cuisine at the most basic level: it provides the oil for cooking the food. In the late nineteenth century, the olive tree was regarded as having almost sacred properties, and a number of poems, short stories, and songs of praise to the olive were published as part of

the upsurge of Provençal nationalism, which is best symbolized by the publications of the poet Frédéric Mistral and his writer friends, the Fé-libres. The revival of Provençal language and culture also applied to the indigenous cuisine.

After the olive the second mainstay of Provençal cuisine is garlic, with tomatoes in third place. Any dish *à la provençale* will almost certainly con-

135

☐

Pages 136–137
Paul Signac, *Still Life*, 1883
Berlin, Nationalgalerie

Here Signac captures the brilliant colors associated
with the south and with the sun itself (alluded to
here in the title of the book in the foreground). These
are forcefully suggested in the yellow, orange, and
pink color combinations.

tain these three ingredients. Aïoli (see recipe), also known as the "butter of Provence," is a regional mayonnaise made more exciting by the addition of garlic—very often in quantities. For Mistral it was a dish representing Provence: "fragrant, gilded like a thread of gold."

Count Curnonsky believed (like many others) that no other part of France could compete with the natural produce of Provence. The aromatic herbs added subtlety and variety to the cooking, providing additional flavor to the meat and game that fed upon them in the wild. The diversity of fruit and vegetables continues to be remarkable. One of the most common vegetables is the artichoke, which is used in a number of different ways, as in Ragoût de Pommes de Terre et de Fonds d'Artichauts à la Provençale (see recipe). Other vegetables typical of the region are zucchini, eggplants, peppers, and fennel, all of which figure in the cuisine. Ratatouille is now probably the best known of the vegetable dishes. Originally from Nice, this dish is typically made with zucchini, eggplant, sweet peppers, and tomatoes simmered in olive oil with herbs. The *tian*, an earthenware ovenproof dish from Provence, is used to prepare dishes made with a variety of vegetables, such as zucchini and tomatoes in Tian de Courgettes et de Tomates (see recipe). Potatoes, artichokes, and spinach may also be used.

In the nineteenth century meat was less frequently part of the staple diet. While sheep (especially the famous Sisteron lambs) and goats provided savory meat and local cheeses, most people lived on soup and vegetables. The vegetables were cooked and served with a vinaigrette and the cooking water could be used as a basis for soup, which varied from the sustaining Soupe au Pistou (see recipe) to the simple Aïgo Boulido (literally "boiled water"). The former is a hearty vegetable and bean soup to which is added a rich pistou sauce of garlic and basil similar to the Italian pesto sauce but without the pine nuts—a reminder of the Italian influence on Provençal cuisine. Aïgo Boulido is made by boiling water with garlic and crushed sage and then pouring it over bread soaked in olive oil. It was the working man's soup, and although today it can also be made with the addition of egg, grated cheese, and spices, one hundred years ago local purists felt that such additions were too bourgeois. A plain simple dish, it was considered ideal for convalescents.

When Vincent van Gogh arrived in Arles in February 1888, it was the simplicity of the food that he commented on, remarking in a letter to his brother Theo that it was the sunshine that sustained him. He had come south filled with ideas of establishing an artists' colony in Provence, the closest European equivalent to that other paradise, Japan.

Today we live in an age where we can visually prepare for travel to foreign or exotic places with the aid of color photography and film. In the nineteenth century this was not the case. Although van Gogh was familiar with the works of Provençal writers such as Alphonse Daudet and admired the Marseillaise artist Monticelli (whose vibrant and colorful paintings he had seen in Paris), nothing prepared him for the ferocity of the sunlight and the vivid yellows and blues that he found there. The latter effects were strikingly captured in his painting *La Maison de Vincent à Arles* (*The Yellow House*). His paintings reflected the colors that he encountered, often mixed with the black and white that he insisted were also colors. He frequently asked Theo to send more money for paints—for him this meant more color—and he wrote in late August to reassure him that he was "hard at it with all the enthusiasm of a Marseillais eating bouillabaisse."

In early August he described to Theo a painting of an all-night café where he ate in the evenings. Since it stayed open throughout the night,

☐

Vincent van Gogh, *La Maison de Vincent à Arles* (*The Yellow House*), 1888
Amsterdam, Foundation Vincent van Gogh

In May 1888 van Gogh rented four rooms at the Yellow House on the Place Lamartine. In this painting of the Yellow House, he is more concerned with describing the harsh Mediterranean light of the Midi, which is emphasized by the juxtaposition of blue with its orange/yellow complementary and the use of thick directional brush strokes to accentuate the color vibrations.

Vincent van Gogh, *The Night Café*, 1888
New Haven, Yale University Art Gallery

Here color is used as a vehicle to express the melancholy and desolation of this all-night café that attracted drunks and down-and-outs. The pervasive greenish coloring adds an eerie note and makes the place seem alien: an effect that is accentuated by the vacant space in the foreground.

Vincent van Gogh, *The Restaurant Carrel at Arles*, c. 1888
Geneva, private collection

When he first arrived in Arles in 1888, van Gogh stayed at the Hotel Carrel, on the rue de la Cavalerie to the north of the town, before moving to the Yellow House.

it attracted those who could not afford to pay for a hotel or had become too drunk to find a place to sleep. Here color is used to paint, as he himself put it, "all the terrible passions of humanity." In *The Night Café* van Gogh communicated a sense of desolation. The seemingly vibrant colors—green, red, yellow, and orange—are held down and mixed with black so that in spite of using such color the overall effect is somber and eerie (due also to the all-pervasive greenish glow). Most of the foreground area is empty: the bare floorboards, empty chairs, and glasses. There is little action—the clients are slumped drunkenly on the marble tabletops. By comparison, *Café Terrace at Night* is a more animated scene of a cafe terrace in the Place du Forum. People are coming and going in the street and sitting on the café terrace. The orange/blue complementaries create an intense effect of artificial light against the deep blue of the night sky.

While Gauguin was in Brittany, van Gogh wrote to him repeatedly asking

Paul Gauguin, *Madame Ginoux at the Café*, 1888
Moscow, Pushkin Museum

Shortly after Gauguin arrived in Arles in 1888, he and van Gogh started work on separate paintings of Madame Ginoux, the proprietor of the Café de la Gare where they frequently drank. Here Gauguin used strong color contrasts to vividly evoke the atmosphere of the café with its billiard table, soda siphon, card game, and smoke fumes.

him to come and join him so that they could set up an artists' colony in the south. At first van Gogh had stayed at the Hôtel Carrel to the north of the town before moving to the Yellow House, where he rented four rooms, the best of which he kept for Gauguin. In his letters to Theo back in Paris, van Gogh communicated his excitement at the prospect of Gauguin's arrival and described his preparations.

When Gauguin arrived they visited van Gogh's favorite cafés together. Each artist painted a portrait of Madame Ginoux, the proprietress of the local station café where the two men drank. In *L'Arlésienne,* van Gogh combined bold coloring with black, a deliberately simplifying and flattening the shapes so that they appear crude. In *Madame Ginoux at the Café* Gauguin uncharacteristically used naturalistic coloring (while van Gogh had situated his version against an abstract, yellow background) and has given us more of a sense of the interior, with drinkers and a billiard table in the background.

However, the two men were completely incompatible. One account even has Gauguin taking over the food preparations, chastising the other artist for his sloppiness in the kitchen and demonstrating how to properly make a salad: precisely slicing the tomatoes and cheese. The gradual deterioration in their relationship, culminating in Gauguin's departure and van Gogh's removal to an asylum at Saint-Rémy, are well documented by the letters of both artists and contemporary accounts.

While van Gogh was an outsider living in Provence, Cézanne was a born and bred southerner. Contemporary descriptions cast him as a stereotypical Provençal peasant: reeking of garlic, dirty, and rude (an image which he seems to have deliberately cultivated when in Paris). Mary Cassatt's description (see Chapter 2), detailing his lack of sophistication at table, does nothing to revise this image. However, she also noted his gentleness and sensitivity.

Cézanne's landscapes of Mont Sainte-Victoire have become so well known that it is difficult to look at this scenery today without being reminded of his paintings. *La Montagne Sainte-Victoire* was a subject that Cézanne returned to many times. In his paintings, the mountain is generally represented from the west, near Cézanne's family home, the Jas de Bouffan. The mountain dominates the composition and Cézanne characteristically simplified its appearance by eliminating unnecessary detail. This profound understanding of the essential structure of the scene in front is combined with animated and interlocking surface brushwork (often in the form of a system of parallel brush strokes), which serves to subtly suggest atmosphere and depth. Cézanne's paring down of natural forms

(often into geometric shapes) involved a rigorous process of simplification, of selection and rejection. He stated that his intention was to approach pictorial problems geometrically, treating nature in terms of the cylinder, sphere, and cone. Here this approach suggests not just the commanding presence of Mont Sainte-Victoire, but also the vast sweep of the plain under shifting Mediterranean light.

Cézanne, whose father had been a hatmaker before becoming a prosperous banker and prominent citizen of Aix-en-Provence, had been

143

Paul Cézanne, *La Montagne Sainte-Victoire*, c. 1887
London, Courtauld Institute Galleries

Cézanne made a number of paintings of this local landmark from the vantage point of the family home, the Jas de Bouffan. The monumentality of the mountain has been suggested by the artist's exclusion of unnecessary detail and by his system of **constructive brush strokes. Recession into space is denoted by the gradual transition from the sharper greens and oranges to the softer blues, mauves, and pinks of the mountain.**

brought up on the local cuisine. The area around Aix was especially famed for its cultivation of vegetables: squash, eggplant, melons, and of course olives. That Cézanne took his native cuisine very seriously is evident in an anecdote that relates how, in the course of a heated family

Paul Cézanne, *Le Déjeuner sur l'herbe*,
1872–1882
Amiens, Musée de Picardie

Cézanne painted a number of versions of this subject. In this one the wide paniered dressed of the women recall eighteenth-century fêtes galantes by artists such as Watteau. Cézanne's lighthearted and airy interpretation is more hedonistic: with the picnickers shown sprawled out in the foreground, dancing or drinking.

discussion that poured scorn on the artist's rascally brother-in-law, Cézanne could find only one good word to say for him: "He knows how to buy olives," an attribute highly prized in Provence.

As well as continually painting the landscape around Aix, Cézanne repeatedly painted the scenery around the coastal village of l'Estaque near Marseilles, giving a forceful impression of lush vegetation and the intensely blue sea and sky that characterized this region. At this time l'Estaque was becoming industrialized, and like van Gogh, Cézanne was not averse to painting both the ugly and the beautiful aspects of this process. In *La Mer à l'Estaque* Cézanne altered and refined the appearance of smokestacks so that they looked like cylinders—a subtle process of idealization at work.

Cézanne's paintings provided a catalyst for many later artists to visit the Midi. When Renoir and Monet made a short trip to the Côte d'Azur in December 1883, they met up with Cézanne in Marseilles. Perennially in search of new motifs, Monet returned on his own to the coast at the beginning of the following year, explaining to his dealer, Durand-Ruel, that while he had enjoyed his pleasure trip with Renoir, he needed to be alone to work from his own impressions. In the 1880s the "common ground" that had existed literally and figuratively between the Impressionists in the 1870s, when they had painted together along the Seine and in Normandy, was no longer relevant to the working process.

In the 1880s and 1890s Monet and Renoir returned to the Midi, often staying at the comfortable hotels built to house the growing numbers of visitors to the Riviera, which was at this time becoming extremely fashionable.

By 1850 many English aristocrats had been spending their winters in Nice, while Lord Brougham had colonized the more exclusive Cannes. This activity intensified after 1860 when Nice officially became part of France and was linked by rail to Marseilles and Toulon and eventually to Menton. The largest group of foreigners were the English, drawn by the climate, the grand hotels, restaurants, and casinos—most notably the casino at Monte Carlo, which was opened in 1857. By the turn of the century the south of France and its amenities figured prominently in gourmet guides to Europe (Auguste Escoffier, the greatest chef of the day, came from Villeneuve in Provence), which listed the culinary attractions of the Riviera in terms of classical French cuisine, not local Provençal cooking. Newnham-Davis's *The Gourmet's Guide to Europe* published in 1903 reiterated a prejudice common in both France and England by advising that only the courageous traveler test the local cuisine: "Those

adventurous souls who wish to eat the fry of sea-urchins and other highly savoury dishes, with strange shell-fish and other extraordinary denizens of the deep as their foundation, should go to Bregaillon's . . . It is necessary to have a liking for garlic and a nose that fears no smells for this adventure."[12] Many wealthy French people also found Provençal cook-

146

□

Gustave Caillebotte, *Melons and Figs*, 1880–1882
Paris, private collection

Caillebotte has suggested the sunshine associated with these summer fruits. The yellows, oranges, and pinks are blended rather than juxtaposed with the mauves, blues, and greens, while he has varied the brushwork in the tablecloth, fruit, and loose coloration of the background to suggest different textures.

ing too coarse and unsophisticated and complained about the ubiquitous
garlic.

Monet returned to Bordighera in early 1884 and spent the winter there
painting. He spent some time also at Menton on the coast, staying at the
Prince of Wales hotel and making twelve or so paintings of the coast and
the view toward Monte Carlo. In 1888 Monet spent some time at Antibes,
where he stayed at a hotel much frequented by artists and recommended
to him by Guy de Maupassant: the Château de la Pinède, perfectly situated at Juan-les-Pins. Here he painted forty canvases (ten of which were
later exhibited in Paris by Theo van Gogh) and wrote enthusiastically to
Gustave Geffroy of the stunning clarity of this "blue" light. He wrote to
Alice Hoschedé of the extraordinary delicacy of the light and color in
which the pinks, whites, and blues had an almost magical quality. He
resolved the difficulty of capturing the intensity and delicate nuances of
southern light by heightening his colors and coordinating warm and cool
tones so that in many of these paintings, such as *Antibes,* he has interwoven greens and blues with oranges, pinks, and reds. Many of these paintings were also reworked later. While conveying transitory effects, they
also have a strong decorative quality (the tree in the foreground of
Antibes, for example), heralding Monet's move away from strict Impressionist ideals.

Renoir too was entranced by the coastal scenery. In the landscapes that

he painted along the Côte d'Azur, he employed loose and silvery tones to suggest the sensuous impact of these exotic places. He returned throughout the 1890s, not only to visit Cézanne but also to continue painting. In spite of the delights of haute cuisine in Nice and Cannes, at home in Provence at Les Collettes, near Cagnes-sur-Mer (where he had settled in 1905) Renoir also appreciated local dishes. The Monets visited him at Les Collettes in 1908 when Monet made his last trip to the Côte d'Azur. Apart from the attractions of the scenery and his desire to see the Renoirs, a further motivation was Aline Renoir's superlative bouilla-

baisse: that quintessentially Mediterranean fish stew made from a range

Pierre-Auguste Renoir, *Strawberries*, 1908 (detail)
Paris, private collection

These strawberries were painted after Renoir bought
land and settled at Collettes, Cagnes-sur-Mer.

of fresh local fish and flavored with saffron, tomatoes, and olive oil, that to this day is a reminder of the quality and variety of the seafood of this region.

Zucchini and Tomato Casserole

Serves 6
- 2 large onions
- 1 lb. eggplant
- 1 lb. zucchini
- 1 lb. tomatoes
- 2 cloves garlic
- 2 teaspoons fresh thyme leaves
- Salt and pepper
- Olive oil

To prepare the vegetables:
Peel and slice the onions, then wash the other vegetables and cut them into slices without peeling.

To make the casserole:
Rub the inside of an ovenproof dish (cast-iron or earthenware) with 1 clove of garlic. Mince the remaining garlic. Lay the vegetables in the dish in alternating layers of onions, eggplant, zucchini, and tomatoes, in that order.

Sprinkle each layer with a little thyme, minced garlic, salt, and pepper, pour over the vegetables a little olive oil. When the dish is full, cover and bake in 300° oven at least 1 hour.

Serve hot as an accompaniment to a rib of beef or grilled lamb chops, or serve cold with a cold roast.

Pesto Soup

This great classic of Provençale cuisine can be prepared with or without white beans. With the beans, it will be close to Italian minestrone. Some people prefer it without the beans because the flavor is then more tart and fresher.

Serves 8
- 1 lb. green beans
- 4 carrots
- 4 potatoes
- 4 tomatoes
- 4 zucchini
- onions
- 2 cups vermicelli
- 4 cloves garlic
- 1 bunch fresh basil
- $\frac{1}{2}$ cup olive oil

Bring 3 quarts water to a boil.

To prepare the vegetables:
Cut off the tips of the beans and cut the beans in half. Peel and dice the carrots and potatoes, peel and seed the tomatoes and cut into small pieces, and slice the zucchini and onion.

To cook:
Drop the vegetables into the boiling water and keep at a low boil 35 to 40 minutes. Add the vermicelli. In a mortar, crush together the garlic and basil, then gradually beat in the olive oil: this mixture is the "pesto" sauce.

When the vermicelli are done, beat half of the pesto sauce into the soup and simmer a few minutes.
Pour into a tureen 1 cup of the soup and the remaining pesto sauce and beat together. Add the rest of the soup and serve at once.

Grand Aïoli

"One should speak the local patois and know how to eat bouillabaisse and garlic, then one would surely find a bourgeois boardinghouse at low cost."
— Vincent van Gogh's letter to Theo (March 18, 1888)

This is a holiday dish, ideal for a summer buffet. It includes meat, fish, vegetables, hard-boiled eggs, and escargots served together with a large bowl of aïoli, a mayonnaise made with olive oil, lemon, and plenty of garlic.

Serves 8
- 4 lbs. codfish fillet, salted and dried
- 2 lbs. tender beef
- 2 lbs. lamb
- 3 doz. "petit gris" escargots, unseasoned in their shells
- Vegetables: 8 carrots, 8 small purple artichokes, 1 lb. good quality green beans, 4 halved fennel heads, 8 potatoes, 8 zucchini, 1 cauliflower, 4 halved leeks, and 1 lb. chick-peas
- 8 whole eggs plus 3 yolks
- 8 cloves fresh firm garlic
- 2 cups good olive oil
- Juice of 1 lemon
- Herbs and spices for the broths: parsley, thyme, bay leaves, fennel seeds, cloves, peppercorns, and 2 small pimentos

The day before:
Soak the cod in a large container filled with fresh water to desalinate the fish. Change the water as often as possible throughout the day.

Soak the chick-peas in a large amount of water.

The rest of the preparation is done the day of serving by poaching the fish and meat, cooking the vegetables, and making the aïoli.

To prepare the cod:
Make a broth with 3 quarts water and half the herbs and spices, then immerse the cod in the cold liquid, bring to a boil, and remove from heat. Let the cod poach in the broth 10 to 15 minutes.

To prepare the meats and vegetables:
Make another broth with 3 quarts water and the remaining herbs and spices, and immerse the beef and lamb in the liquid, bring to a boil, and cook on medium heat 1 hour. In a separate pot of water, boil the potatoes in their skins with a bay leaf until done. Cook the artichokes separately. Twenty minutes before the meat is done, add the remaining vegetables to the broth.

To prepare the escargots:
The escargots have to be cooked at the last minute. Make a broth with thyme and cook the escargots 25 minutes. Meanwhile, hard-boil 8 eggs, peel, and halve lengthwise.

To make the aïoli:
In a mortar, crush the garlic with a pestle into a fine purée, then add 3 egg yolks, salt, and pepper and blend. Slowly pour the oil into the mixture in a thin continuous stream, beating vigorously with a

wooden spoon. The mixture must
be completely smooth. If the oil
doesn't blend in easily, stop pouring
at once and beat vigorously until
completely absorbed.
Once the mayonnaise has thickened,
add the lemon juice. Fresh aïoli is
quite creamy and should be
prepared just before serving.

To serve:
Arrange the fish and meat on
separate dishes and surround with
the vegetables, the hard-boiled eggs,
and the escargots. Set the mortar of
aïoli in the center. The diversity of
the ingredients allows for attractive
and appetizing displays.

Provençale Stew with Potatoes and Artichoke Hearts

Serves 4 to 6
- 1½ lbs. potatoes (6 to 7 medium)
- 1 lb. artichoke hearts
- 3 tomatoes
- 3 cloves garlic
- ½ cup olive oil
- ½ cup meat juice
- Thyme leaves
- 1 bay leaf
- Salt and pepper

To prepare the vegetables:
Wash, peel, and slice the potatoes. Remove the leaves and "whiskers" of the artichokes and keep only the hearts. Cut into thin slices.

Peel and crush the tomatoes, and peel and mince the garlic.

To cook:
Heat the oil in a cast-iron casserole, then sauté the potatoes and artichoke hearts and add the garlic and tomatoes. Moisten with the meat juice. Add the thyme and bay leaves.
Cover and simmer on very low heat 1 hour, stirring occasionally so the vegetables don't stick to the bottom. Season with salt and pepper, and serve hot or lukewarm.

Grilled Fresh Sardines in Salt

This is a very simple and delicious recipe from the fishermen of the Mediterranean coast. It should be cooked and eaten outdoors.

Serves 4
- 12 large fresh sardines
- 12 leaves fresh basil
- Freshly ground pepper
- ½ cup or more coarse salt
- 4 sweet red onions, sliced (one per person)

Prepare a barbecue of hot coals. Scale and clean the fish, and wash in plenty of water. Sprinkle the inside with fresh pepper and stuff with one basil leaf. Set aside. Crush the salt with a pestle and carefully roll each sardine in the salt. Grill sardines 4 inches above the coals, 3 to 4 minutes on each side.
Serve hot with slices of sweet red onions.

NOTES

1. Auguste Vollard, *Recollections of a Picture Dealer* (London: Constable, 1936), 151–155; Denvir, 89.
2. Ibid.
3. John Rewald. *Paul Cézanne* (Paris: Flammarion, 1986), 174.
4. Émile Zola, *L'Oeuvre* (Paris: Charpentier, 1886), 78–79.
5. George M. Musgrave, *A Ramble through Normandy* (London: David Bogne, 1855).
6. Marie-Ernest Richardin, *La Cuisine française* (Paris: 1907), 112.
7. George Moore, *Reminiscences of the Impressionist Painters* (Dublin, 1906).
8. Alfred Delvau, *Histoire anecdotique des cafés et cabarets de Paris* (Paris, 1862).
9. Edmond de Goncourt, *Journal Mémoires de la vie littéraire* (Monaco: R. Ricatte, 1956).
10. Gaston Poulain, *Bazille et ses amis* (Paris: La Renaissance du Livre, 1932), 130.
11. Ibid., 40–41.
12. Lt.-Col. Newnham-Davis, *The Gourmet's Guide to Europe* (London: Grant Richards, 1903).

PHOTO CREDITS